Witnesses to the Ends
of the Earth

WITNESSES TO THE ENDS OF THE EARTH

NEW TESTAMENT REFLECTIONS ON MISSION

FRANCIS J. MOLONEY, SDB

Paulist Press
New York / Mahwah NJ

Cover Image: *Pentecost;* painting by the late Edgardo de Guzman. Used with permission.

Cover design by Sharyn Banks
Book design by Domenika Fairy

First published in 2020 by St. Paul's Publications, Strathfield, Australia © Francis J. Moloney, SDB, 2020. This edition published in the United States in 2022 by Paulist Press.

All rights reserved. No part of this publication may be reproduced, stored in a retrieval system, or transmitted in any form or by any means, electronic, mechanical, photocopying, recording, scanning, or otherwise, without either the prior written permission of the Publisher, or authorization through payment of the appropriate per-copy fee to the Copyright Clearance Center, Inc., www.copyright.com. Requests to the Publisher for permission should be addressed to the Permissions Department, Paulist Press, permissions@paulistpress.com.

The publishers gratefully acknowledge permission to include the following material in this book:

Chapter 1: Excerpt adapted from *Reading the New Testament in the Church* by Francis J. Moloney, copyright © 2015. Used by permission of Baker Academic, a division of Baker Publishing Group.

Chapter 5: Excerpt adapted from *Love in the Gospel of John* by Francis J. Moloney, copyright © 2013. Used by permission of Baker Academic, a division of Baker Publishing Group.

Library of Congress Cataloging-in-Publication Data
Names: Moloney, Francis J, author.
Title: Witnesses to the ends of the earth : New Testament reflections on mission / Francis J Moloney, SDB.
Description: Strathfield, Australia ; New York : St Pauls, 2022. | Includes bibliographical references. | Summary: "Eminent biblical scholar, Francis J. Moloney, SDB, explores the teaching on mission found in the letters of St. Paul, the Gospels of Mark and Matthew, Luke-Acts, and the Gospel of John, showing how each inspired author provides unique yet complementary insights into the mission entrusted to the followers of Jesus-a mission ad intra (to the community) and ad Gentes (to the wider world)"– Provided by publisher.
Identifiers: LCCN 2021035627 | ISBN 9780809155910 (paperback)
Subjects: LCSH: Missions–Biblical teaching. | Bible. New Testament–Criticism, interpretation, etc.
Classification: LCC BV2073 .M57 2022 | DDC 266–dc23
LC record available at https://lccn.loc.gov/2021035627

ISBN 978-0-8091-5591-0 (paperback)
ISBN 978-1-58768-994-9 (e-book)

Published by Paulist Press
997 Macarthur Boulevard
Mahwah, New Jersey 07430
www.paulistpress.com

Printed and bound in the
United States of America

CONTENTS

Preface vii

Abbreviations x

1. The Pauline Mission: "The power of the resurrection"
   (Phil 3:10) 1

2. The Gospel of Mark: The Twelve, Mission, and Failure:
   "He is going before you into Galilee" (Mark 16:7) 27

3. The Gospel of Matthew: The Turning Point of the Ages:
   "Make disciples of all nations" (Matt 28:19) 53

4. The Gospel of Luke and the Acts of the Apostles:
   Empowered by the Spirit, Witnesses to the Ends of the Earth
   (Luke 24:47-49; Acts 1:8) 79

5. The Gospel of John: The Foundation of the Church
   and Its Mission: "'It is finished.' Then he bowed his head and
   handed down the Spirit" (John 19:30) 109

6. The Celebration of the Eucharist at the Heart of the
   Christian Mission: "As often as you shall eat this bread and
   drink this cup, you proclaim the Lord's death until he comes"
   (1 Cor 11:26) 129

Epilogue 145

Bibliography 153

PREFACE

The reflections that follow have two sources. In the first place, I began to write them in response to the request of the Pontifical Missionary Society and the Pontifical Missionary Union of the Catholic Church in Vietnam. They were delivered and generously received in two seminars conducted in the Diocesan Pastoral Centre in Vung Tau from 30 June until 6 July 2019. I developed them further for presentations at two other seminars, delivered at the Don Bosco Retreat Centre, Hua Hin, Thailand, from 13 to 19 October 2019, the result of an invitation from the Thai Province of the Salesians of Don Bosco. From the beginnings of the Christian tradition, proclaiming what God has done for humankind in and through Jesus Christ, both within one's immediate surroundings (mission *ad intra*) and among people of other nations and cultures (mission *ad Gentes*), has been part of its agenda. The Apostle Paul is eloquent proof of that truth.[1]

The second source for the reflections is my 50 years of experience studying, teaching, and writing about the New Testament.[2] People aware of my work over the past half-century will find much that is familiar in what follows. I have drawn heavily from earlier studies

---

1   Missionary activity is an important part of the Christian witness "at home." This is regularly referred to via the Latin expression *missio ad intra*. *Missio ad Gentes* is an expression used to describe the traditional meaning of "missionary activity," sending Christian missionaries to various parts of the non-Christian world to preach and witness to the Gospel.

2   I will use the English translation of the Bible from the New Revised Standard Version (NRSV), except where I have provided my own translation. I will indicate my occasional "author's translations" with the abbreviation AT.

upon Paul and the four Gospels. But this is the first time I have focused my attention upon the New Testament theme of mission that emerges forcibly from our Sacred Scriptures.

The conclusions I draw at the end of each New Testament reflection on the Christian mission, and in the summary of the Epilogue, devoting special attention to the resurrection of Jesus as the birth of the Church's mission, are my own ... but they are consistent with a long-standing part of the Christian missionary tradition. Some detailed elements in the studies that follow have appeared in more specialized books and essays. I have attempted to keep scholarly notes to a minimum. However, my own original publications, and other relevant details, appear in the footnotes. From time to time I also use the footnotes to direct the reader to other helpful literature.[3]

The reflections that follow on the missionary vocation of all Christians have a specific focus. *Basic to the Christian's missionary vocation is the missionary vocation of Jesus of Nazareth.* That theme deserves a book of its own. My own earlier study of the mission of Jesus in the Fourth Gospel alone fills 32 pages![4] In what follows, occasional necessary reference is made to the primacy of the mission of Jesus, but the invitations from Vietnam and Thailand that generated this book required that I spoke of the mission of the disciples of Jesus (then and now!). My focus, therefore, is almost entirely upon those disciples whose stories appear in the New Testament texts, and the myriad of further Christian disciples who have been inspired by them through the centuries.

---

[3] I am grateful to the various editors and publishing houses, indicated in those notes, who have allowed further use of my earlier research and writing for the purposes of this book.

[4] Interested readers should consult the older, but very valuable, study of Donald Senior and Carroll Stuhlmueller, *The Biblical Foundations for Mission* (Maryknoll, NY: Orbis Books, 1983). This comprehensive study considers both Old and New Testament "foundations" for mission. On the mission of Jesus, see pp. 141-60. For my study of the mission of Jesus in the Fourth Gospel, see Francis J. Moloney, *Love in the Gospel of John. An Exegetical, Literary, and Theological Study* (Grand Rapids: Baker Academic, 2013), 37-69.

It has been a privilege to address these issues in two "missionary" countries. Vietnam, with its own challenges of living and preaching Christianity in a secular and Communist society, is one of the largest providers of missionaries *ad Gentes* in the contemporary Roman Catholic Church. Thailand is still on the "receiving end" of the Church's missionary activity *ad Gentes*.[5] The enthusiasm and joy I have experienced in these Asian nations have been a source of encouragement to me. I am grateful that the requests of my close neighbors have led me to think, speak, discuss, and write about our Christian mission.

> *Francis J. Moloney, SDB, AM, FAHA*
> *Catholic Theological College, University of Divinity*
> *Melbourne, Victoria, AUSTRALIA*

---

[5] See the most informative study of Robert Costet, *Pax Hominibus. A History of the Mission of Siam and Laos*, trans. and ed. Apisake Monthienvichienchai (Bangkok: Catholic Social Communication of Thailand, 2019).

ABBREVIATIONS

AT	Author's Translation
ATF	Australian Theological Foundation
BCE	Before the Common Era (traditionally BC)
c.	approximately (from the Latin "circa")
CE	Common Era (traditionally AD)
LXX	The Septuagint (the Greek translation of the Hebrew Bible)
PL	*Patrologia Latina* (= *Patrologiae cursus completes. Series Latina*). Edited by Jacques-Paul Migne. 217 vols. Paris: Migne, 1844-1864.
s.v.	sub voce (i.e., under the word in a dictionary entry)

BIBLICAL ABBREVIATIONS

OLD TESTAMENT

Exod	Exodus
Num	Numbers
Deut	Deuteronomy
Ps	Psalms
Isa	Isaiah
Ezek	Ezekiel
Dan	Daniel
Hag	Haggai
Zech	Zechariah
Mal	Malachi
Wis	Wisdom

NEW TESTAMENT

Matt	Matthew
Acts	Acts of the Apostles
Rom	Romans
1 Cor	1 Corinthians
2 Cor	2 Corinthians
Gal	Galatians
Phil	Philippians
1 Thess	1 Thessalonians
2 Tim	2 Timothy
Phlm	Philemon
Rev	Revelation

1

THE PAULINE MISSION

"The power of the resurrection" (Phil 3:10)

The First Letter to the Thessalonians may have been written as early as 49-50 CE. Less than 20 years after the death and resurrection of Jesus someone had begun to forge an understanding of what God had done for humankind in and through Jesus of Nazareth that remains, to this day, the bedrock of the Christian theological and spiritual tradition.[1] As we will see, Mark, Matthew, Luke, and John report Jesus' instructions that the Gospel of Jesus Christ must be preached to all the nations (see Mark 13:10; Matt 28:16-20; Luke 24:46-49; Acts 1:8; John 17:1-26). Jesus himself was aware that he was not the master of his own destiny, but that he was on a God-directed mission, "sent" to bring the good news wherever he went during his wandering ministry in Galilee (Mark 1:38-39), Judea (Luke 9:51–19:44), Tyre and Sidon, and in the Gentile world on the other side of the Jordan (Mark 7:24–8:10). The Apostle of the Gentiles regularly describes the

---

1 On this, see Raymond E. Brown, *An Introduction to the New Testament*, Anchor Bible Reference Library (New York: Doubleday, 1997), 456-66. On 1 Thess 1:1-10, Brown comments: "With the opening ten verses one would hear references to God the Father, the Lord Jesus Christ, and the Holy Spirit, and to faith, love and hope. That is a remarkable testimony to how quickly ideas that became standard in Christianity were already in place."

urgency and the nature of his vocation to preach: "Woe to me if I do not proclaim the Gospel" (1 Cor 9:16. See 1 Cor 1:26-31; 2 Cor 2:1-5), to be ambassador of the Gospel (5:19-21. See Rom 10:14-21).

The seed of all that is to follow in his missionary letters can be found in 1 Thessalonians 1:9-10: "How you turned to God from idols, to serve a living and true God, and to wait for his Son from heaven, whom he raised from the dead, Jesus who delivers us from the wrath to come." The following chapter reflects upon a central element in the Pauline understanding of what God did for us in and through his Son.[2] Paul was so overwhelmed by the message of the Gospel, that he could do no other than spend his life, walking thousands of kilometers to all parts of the Roman Empire, to preach his message, and then to further remind and instruct the communities through his writings, the fruit and an ongoing form of his evangelizing mission.[3] There are many elements in Paul's message, and much that he contributed to developing Christianity, but for our purposes, we will focus upon a *key to reading Paul that indicates the passion of his missionary activity.*

Most reflections upon Paul's missionary activities that trace where he went and what he did make the understandable mistake of following the three journeys as they are reported in the second half of the Acts of the Apostles. He makes the first journey into Galatia and Asia Minor (Acts 13:1–14:28). The second takes him through Troas into Europe: Philippi, Thessalonica, Beroea, Athens and Corinth (15:36–18:22). His final third journey is dominated by his troubled presence in Ephesus, and his farewell speech in Miletus (18:23–21:17). Trials

---

[2] For an earlier version of what follows, without the focus upon mission, see Francis J. Moloney, *Reading the New Testament in the Church. A Primer for Pastors, Religious Educators, and Believers* (Grand Rapids: Baker Academic, 2015), 91-112.

[3] The modern and contemporary world has lost all sense of the "personal presence" communicated in antiquity by means of a letter. In many ways, Paul remains present to his communities by means of his amazing letter-writing.

at the hands of both Jews and Romans (21:18–26:32) lead to his final journey to Rome (27:1–28:31). Such a portrait can be misleading. Although the author of the Acts of the Apostles, known to us as Luke, certainly reported many events from the earliest years of the existence of a Christian community and its mission, like all historians of his time he uses that data for his own purposes. He wishes to portray the unstoppable spread of God's word from Jerusalem to Rome, and beyond, the result of the driving power of the Spirit.[4]

If we wish to come to grips with Paul's personal assessment of his missionary passion, it is best that we turn to his own letters. Thus, in what follows, we will focus our attention on *what he wrote*. This is not to say that there is nothing of value in the Lucan description of Paul and his mission.[5] However, the best place to discover what Paul said is within the pages of his own writings. I will focus upon some major Pauline texts, in the hope that a close reading of these passages will provide something of a key for a reading of the Pauline corpus, the fruit of his inspiring missionary vocation. Paul, the devout Jew, had been so transformed by the "power of the resurrection" that he rethought the universal acceptance of God's glorious presence *at the beginning* that would only return *at the end*. With the death and resurrection of Jesus, "a new creation" has broken into the human story. This is the message that drove Paul to the ends of the earth, and to martyrdom.

There is no doubt that Paul was a remarkable missionary. In a moment of what he calls weakness, in a necessary explanation to the Corinthians who were doubting his credentials as an apostle and a

---

4   On this, see the essay "The Gospel of Luke and the Acts of the Apostles: Empowered by the Spirit, Witnesses to the Ends of the Earth," on pp. 79-107, below. However doubtful some of the chronological sequences and precision in the speeches might be in the Acts of the Apostles, they are reliable evidence of Paul as a remarkable missionary.

5   See the balanced assessment of Mikael C. Parsons, *Luke: Storyteller, Interpreter, Evangelist* (Peabody, MA: Hendrickson, 2007), 123-37.

missionary, he describes some of the experiences he was prepared to undergo, in order to bring the Gospel to the ends of the earth:

> Are they Hebrews? So am I. Are they Israelites? So am I. Are they ministers of Christ? I am talking like a madman – I am a better one with far greater labors, far more imprisonments, with countless floggings, and often near death. Five times I have received from the Jews the forty lashes minus one. Three times I was beaten with rods. Once I received a stoning. Three times I was shipwrecked; for a night and a day I was adrift at sea; on frequent journeys, in danger from rivers, danger from bandits, danger from my own people, danger from Gentiles, danger in the city, danger in the wilderness, danger at sea, danger from false brothers and sisters; in toil and hardship, through many a sleepless night, hungry and thirsty, often without food, cold and naked. (2 Cor 11:22-27)

In a parallel passage, where Paul again dwells upon his preparedness to endure hardships, he explains why:

> For his sake I have suffered the loss of all things, and I regard them as rubbish that I may gain Christ and be found in him, not having a righteousness of my own that comes from the law, but one that comes through faith in Christ, the righteousness from God based on faith. I want to know Christ *and the power of his resurrection and the sharing of his sufferings by becoming like him in his death, if somehow I may attain the resurrection from the dead.* (Phil 3:8-11)

THE POWER OF THE RESURRECTION

Paul provides us with some important information about the encounter with the risen Lord that led to his so-called "conversion." He tells us that he was a Jew "of the people of Israel, of the tribe of Benjamin, a Hebrew born of Hebrews" (Phil 3:5. See also Rom 11:1; 2 Cor 11:22). He also tells us that he belonged to the Jewish sect of the Pharisees (Phil 3:5). This reasonably recent sect within the larger religious body known to us as Judaism sought to practice a radical holiness. They adhered carefully to every aspect of the Torah: both its written code, and the various oral interpretations of the written Law that had emerged and were emerging as Israel attempted to make the Torah apply to a changing society and its practices. Luke informs us that Paul was educated to his Pharisaism in Jerusalem by Gamaliel (Acts 22:3), the rabbi made famous in Christian tradition for his wise advice about allowing the new Christian movement to run free, either to failure if it was a mere human creation, or to flourish if it was of God (Acts 5:35-39). Some doubt this link: Gamaliel was prepared to be patient with this new Jewish sect, allowing it to run its course, or fail as so many other sects had failed. Saul had no such patience. He zealously wished to rid Judaism of this heretical group.

Paul himself tells us nothing of that background, but he regularly admits that his passion for the Law and its observance led him to a "zeal" that could not tolerate the emerging form of sectarian Judaism claiming that the crucified Jesus of Nazareth was the Christ. His repeated descriptions of his former life as a persecutor of the earliest Church (Phil 3:6; Gal 1:13, 23; 1 Cor 15:9) indicate his desire to make it clear that something dramatic and almost beyond description broke into his life. It led to a reversal of his understanding of the way the Law was to be understood and lived, and his understanding of Jesus as the Christ. Paul was transformed by what we might nowadays call a "religious experience," some form of "out of body" experience that changed the direction of his life to such an extent that he spent the rest of his days, even to the point of ultimate martyrdom, in a passionate gift of himself to preaching the Gospel, as he came to understand it.[6] As he tells the Corinthians, "For if I preach the gospel, that gives me no grounds for boasting. For necessity is laid upon me. Woe to me if I do not preach the gospel" (1 Cor 9:16), and the Romans: "I am under obligation both to Greeks and to barbarians, both to the wise and the foolish: so I am eager to preach the gospel to you also who are in Rome" (Rom 1:14-15). Paul was the first of the great missionaries, and he has had many wonderful followers. What follows reflects upon *why he was* such a passionate missionary, and *what he preached*.

The Lucan presentation of that transformative experience is well known. In fact, in the Acts of the Apostles Paul tells of his Damascus experience three times (Acts 9:1-30; 22:3-21; 26:9-23). Paul's own direct testimony is less descriptive, but more theologically impressive. There is no journey to Damascus, no falling from a horse (he fell to the ground [Acts 9:4]), no voice from heaven, no blindness and no mention of Straight Street and Ananias. What Paul does tell us, however, is that he experienced a "sight" of the risen Jesus, and that this revelation was the foundation of his call to be an apostle of Jesus Christ to the Gentiles (see 1 Cor 9:1; 15:8; Gal 1:12-16). Paul confirms that this experience took place near Damascus (Gal 1:17; 2 Cor 11:32), but the geography does not interest him. Scholars debate how "immediate" Paul's transformation was, and whether he spent several years assimilating his experience and developing his Gospel.

---

6   We have no first-hand witness to the martyrdom of Paul. There are hints in the Acts of the Apostles that he died in Rome (see Acts 20:22-25, 37-38; 21:11, 13), and tradition holds that he was executed in 67 CE, during the persecution of Christians under the Emperor Nero. For a brief "life of Paul," see Sherri Brown and Francis J. Moloney, *Interpreting the New Testament* (Grand Rapids: Eerdmans, 2019), 151-59.

They also discuss whether Paul experienced a "conversion" or a "call." This is an important distinction, as many would say that underlying Paul's zeal as a Jew and his zeal as a Christian was a single-minded passion for the one true God that was always with him. His passion for God was not changed by means of a conversion, but he experienced a "call" from that God to recognize and proclaim what God had done for humankind in and through his Son.[7] His passion for the God of Israel never wavered, but his acceptance of Jesus' role in God's action in our world and in human history transformed him. As his zeal for the one and only true God of Israel sent him on a mission to cleanse a holy people from a heretical sect, his experience of the risen Christ developed into an equally zealous mission to proclaim what God had done for *all people* through the death and resurrection of Jesus.

Returning to the brief autobiographical passage that I have already cited, Paul provided a pen-picture of his transformation from a zealous Jew to a passionate Christian missionary:

> For his sake I have suffered the loss of all things, and count them as refuse, in order that I may gain Christ and be found in him, not having a righteousness of my own based on law, but that which is through faith in Christ, the righteousness from God that depends on faith; that I may know him and **the power of his resurrection**, and may share his sufferings, becoming like him in his death, that if possible I may attain the resurrection from the dead. (Phil 3:7-11. See also 1 Cor 1:18; 2 Cor 4:7; 12:9; 13:4)

For Paul, and for the Gospel that he preached, the only things that mattered were:

---

[7] For a summary of this debate, see David G. Horrell, *An Introduction to the Study of Paul*, 2nd ed. (London: T. & T. Clark, 2006), 29-31.

- To know Christ Jesus as Lord
- To gain Christ and to be found in him
- To have right relationship (righteousness) with God through belief in what God has done for us in and through Jesus Christ
- To reject any idea that such a relationship can be generated by anything human, such as the observance of restrictive practices associated with the Law
- To live and die as Jesus of Nazareth lived and died, becoming like him in suffering and death
- To eventually share in Jesus' resurrection from the dead

The source for Paul's relentless and passionate conviction and missionary activity that these are the only things that matter is *the power of the resurrection that drove his missionary activity.*

It is well known that Paul tells us little of the life of Jesus. If the only written documents we had from the beginnings of Christianity were the letters of Paul, we would only know that in the fullness of time, Jesus was born of a woman (Gal 4:4), that the night before he died he celebrated a meal with his disciples that looked to his suffering, death and ultimate victory through resurrection for its meaning (1 Cor 11:23-26), and that he was crucified, buried, raised, and seen by a multitude of witnesses (1 Cor 15: 1-8). The last of these witnesses, the one untimely and unworthily born, was Paul himself (15:8-9). Although there are echoes of Jesus' teachings insinuated into the letters, we have no "narrative" of the life of Jesus. For Paul, writing so close to those events, what had to become the heart of his preaching was Jesus' death and resurrection. As he tells us, in his First Letter to the Corinthians:

> For Jews demand signs and Greeks seek wisdom, but we preach Christ crucified, a stumbling block to Jews and folly to Gentiles, but to those who are called, both Jews and Greeks, Christ the power of God and the wisdom of God. For the foolishness of God is wiser than men, and the weakness of God is stronger than men. (1 Cor 1:22-25)

At the heart of the Pauline Gospel is his explanation of how crucifixion is transformed into power and wisdom, weakness into strength. The power and the wisdom of God are manifested in what Paul has called "the power of the resurrection."

ADAM AND CHRIST – ROMANS 5:12-21

To explain how Jesus' death and resurrection, a stumbling-block and folly, is the power and wisdom of God (see 1 Cor 1:22-25), Paul develops a unique understanding of God's threefold intervention within the history of humankind:

1. At creation,
2. During the span of the human story in the life, death and resurrection of Jesus,
3. At the end of time.

On only two occasions does Paul use the expression "a new creation," and he does so without any explanation. He seems to take it for granted that his readers and listeners know what he means when he tells the Galatians, troubled by whether or not they should retain or abandon former Jewish practices: "For neither circumcision counts for anything, nor uncircumcision, but a new creation" (Gal 6:15). He instructs the Corinthians, "Anyone in Christ is a new creation. The old has passed away; behold the new has come" (2 Cor 5:17). Paul is not quite as blunt here. He informs the Corinthians that "life in Christ" generates a new creation. This theme calls for further exploration. We must notice the *universal nature* of the newness that the events of Jesus Christ has brought. It is a "new creation"; an action of God that transforms our understanding of the nature and purpose of the creation of humankind and the whole of the natural world.

A crucial text for our investigation appears in Romans 5:12-21.[8] Here we find Paul's conviction that in and through the death and resurrection of Jesus we have a new creation. Like all Jews, Paul accepted that "in the beginning" (Gen 1:1) everything was exactly as God wanted it. In that story, Adam was a key player. Paul took the story of Adam and Eve as an account of how things happened. First-century Jews knew nothing of modern and contemporary source and redaction criticism of the Pentateuch. God's glory and God's will were evident in the perfect order and beauty of creation and in the lives of Adam and Eve.[9]

However, sin entered the world through the *disobedience* of Adam, and once sin had begun, it gradually spread and took possession of the whole of God's originally perfect creation: "Sin came into the world through one man, and death came through sin, and so death spread to all because all have sinned" (v. 12). What is being affirmed here is that the disobedience of Adam, as told in the biblical story of creation, had a *universal effect*. The earth rebels, the animals rebel, tension, difficulty and misunderstanding develops between men and women (see Gen 3:14-24). Because of the sin of *one person*, death and sin enters creation

---

[8] See Brendan J. Byrne, *Romans*, Sacra Pagina 6 (Collegeville: Liturgical Press, 1996), 173-87.

[9] On the irrelevance of "what actually happened" to generate sin in the world, and the importance of the "truth" communicated by the *biblical story* of Adam and Eve, see James D. G. Dunn, *Romans*, 2 vols., Word Biblical Commentary 38a-b (Dallas, TX: Word Books, 1988), 1:289-90.

and the human condition *universally*. *Everyone sinned*.¹⁰ Long after the universal spread of death and sin, God gave the Law to Moses. Sin continued to abound because the Law could not free us from the slavery of sin. It could protect us ... but not save us (v. 13).¹¹

The tragedy of the disobedience of Adam "at the beginning" was crucial for the Jewish understanding of human history. Paul, along with his Jewish contemporaries, believed that final salvation and the restoration of a world as God had made it, full of God's glory, the restoration of a situation of right relationship between God and all creation, would take place only "at the end" of all time. God would restore everything to its original beauty. Jewish tradition maintained that the loss of God's glory in the world because of the sin of Adam, at the *beginning* of all time, would return in the restoration of God's glory *at the end* of all time.¹² The glory of God that was in existence at the beginning of all time would be restored by God at the end of all time. As the scholars say in German, their favorite language, the *Urzeit* would return at the *Endzeit*. God's glory, present at the beginning of time, would be restored by the action of God at the end of time.

But in Romans 5:14, in his description of the tragic universal presence of death and sin, Paul introduces a note of hope. He refers to Adam as "a type of the one who was to come." What this means for the

---

10 Scholarship has long debated the use of the difficult Greek expression *ephōi* in v. 12. Following Byrne (*Romans*, 177, 183), I regard it as an indication of "an emphatic causal expression" (p. 177).

11 Over recent years, our understanding of Paul's theological (and pastoral) attitude to "the Law" has undergone dramatic revision. Seminal to this were Ed Parish Sanders, *Paul and Palestinian Judaism. A Comparison of Patterns of Religion* (Philadelphia: Fortress, 1977). See also Brendan Byrne, "Interpreting Romans Theologically in a Post - 'New Perspective' Perspective," *Harvard Theological Review* 94 (2001): 227-41; Idem, "The Problem of *Nomos* and the Relationship with Judaism in Romans," *The Catholic Biblical Quarterly* 62 (2000): 294-309.

12 See Robin Scroggs, *The Last Adam. A Study in Pauline Anthropology* (Oxford: Basil Blackwell, 1966).

human story is told in vv. 15-16. Adam is "a type" of the one who is to come, Jesus Christ, because his *disobedience* had *universal consequences* (vv. 12-13). Paul reverses that story with his strong adversative "but" at the beginning of v. 15 (*all'ouk*). God's graciousness has bestowed upon us a "free gift." The similarity with Adam, "a type" of the one who is to come, is that the *obedience* of the one who was to come, a gracious gift of God, had *universal consequences*. As we have already seen, God had transformed Paul by sweeping him up into the power of Jesus' death and resurrection. Another similarity between Adam and Christ is that the sin of Adam took place as an event in human history, just as the obedience, death and resurrection of Jesus of Nazareth took place as an event in human history. Sin entered history in and through Adam; God's gift of grace entered history in and through Jesus Christ. Although the effects of the sin of Adam and the effects of the death and resurrection of Jesus are equally universal, they are radically opposed: Adam's sin brought condemnation; Jesus' obedience brought justification, the possibility of a right relationship with God. God's free-gift of grace offered to us in and through Jesus Christ overcomes the dominance of sin and death (vv. 16-17).

Paul's mission, as reflected throughout his letters was determined by his passionate belief that the Jewish view of history, leaving us in chaos and sin, protected but not saved by the Law, had been transformed.[13] The death and resurrection of Jesus, the free-gift of God to a sinful world, opened up a new possibility for the whole of humankind. We do not have to wait for the end of time for God's way in the world to be re-established. God broke into the passage of ordinary human time in and through Jesus Christ. Jesus reversed

---

13 As an unknown Hellenistic Jew wrote late in the second century before Christ: "In his wisdom the legislator (Moses) ... surrounded us with unbroken palisades and iron walls to prevent our mixing with the other peoples in any matter, being thus kept pure in body and soul, preserved from false belief, and worshiping the only God omnipotent over all creation" (*Letter of Aristeas* 139). Text in James H. Charlesworth, *The Old Testament Pseudepigrapha*, 2 vols. (New York: Doubleday, 1985), 2:22.

Adam's sin of disobedience by means of his unconditional obedience to God. Because of Jesus' death and resurrection, therefore, what Jewish tradition described as a future event, to take place *only at the end* of all time, was *already* happening: "Therefore just as one man's trespass led to condemnation for all, so one man's act of righteousness leads to justification and life for all. For as by the one man's disobedience the many were made sinners, so by the one man's obedience the many will be made righteous" (vv. 18-19).

The Pauline use of the expression "made righteous" means that "right relationship" can now exist between God and the human condition.[14] Union with God and a fullness of life are now available. What Jesus had done for us introduced a "new creation." The first creation had been marred by sin and disobedience, the new creation is marked by the free-gift of God that produces life, through the obedience of one man, Jesus Christ (v. 17). The beauty of God's original creation had been disfigured by sin. It has been restored in the new creation made possible by obedience unto death and the resurrection of Jesus. What was wrecked by one man's disobedience has been restored by another man's obedience. But what happens in and through God's gift of his Son is not just restoration. Its grace-filled effects abundantly surpass the consequences of Adam's sin. This message is stated over and over: one man's trespass led to condemnation, one man's act of righteousness leads to life (v. 18), one man's disobedience leads to sin, one man's obedience leads to righteousness (v. 19), the Law made us conscious of sin, but did not free us; but where sin increased, grace abounded all the more (v. 20). The life that we have through Jesus Christ is eternal life (v. 21).

Despite the beauty and clarity of this teaching, Paul the missionary was a realist. Our missionary activity must follow him in his realism. The sinful condition established by the sin of Adam has not

---

14 See Byrne, *Romans*, 57-60.

disappeared. It was patently obvious in the world of Paul as it is in our own time that sin still reigns in the hearts of many, and increasingly in many human institutions. The ruination of the original creation that let loose sin and death in the world is still abroad. It runs side by side with the grace and freedom established in the new creation made possible in Jesus Christ. We are called to choose which story we would like to join: that of Adam, or that of Jesus Christ. A choice lies before us, both individually and collectively: "Which story are you going to let be told in your life, in your world? Are you choosing death with Adam or life with Christ?" All forms of disobedience, selfishness, exploitation, and even the attitude of "going it alone" apart from God, no matter how well intentioned, ranges one inevitably on the side of Adam. Surrender to God's gift of righteousness through faith leads to life and to becoming, with Christ, in imitation of his obedience to God, an instrument of life.

The call to "conversion," even (and perhaps sometimes especially) for the baptized, remains an essential part of our missionary mandate. Paul does not abandon his traditional Jewish understanding of the course of history. The return of God at the end of all time is still firmly in place.[15] It remains an essential part of Christian thought and preaching. The difference now is that we do not have to wait for the end of time to encounter the glory of God in our lives. *The universal relevance of this core element in the Pauline message drives Paul into mission. This is not something that can be restricted to a nation or a people.* It is *universally* available through faith in Christ manifested, as we will see shortly, in our living as Jesus Christ lived, putting on Christ. For Paul, we still "wait for his Son from heaven, whom he raised from the dead, Jesus who delivers us from the wrath to come" (1 Thess 1:10). As Brendan Byrne puts it:

---

[15] See the good summary and the helpful diagram in Horrell, *An Introduction to the Study of Paul*, 69-73.

You have been part of the Adam story; your human history is marked by its consequences. Do you wish to let the Christ story and its (more powerful) consequences be the final story told in your life and in your world?[16]

HAVE THE SAME MIND AS CHRIST JESUS – PHILIPPIANS 2:5-11

Further clarification comes from one of our best loved Pauline passages, strongly present in the Liturgy, especially powerful in Holy Week, and even set to music in a number of attractive variations, the so-called "hymn" of Philippians 2:5-11. This unforgettable synthesis of the passage of the Christ from his pre-existent situation of equality with God to a further place where he is Lord of all to the glory of God the Father, via the total emptying of himself in death, death even on a cross, instructs us *how* the new creation came about. Setting the hymn within the Letter to the Philippians leads us further: how are we, in our own turn, swept into the new creation?

Our reflection upon Romans 5:12-21 insisted, via the type and antitype of Adam and Christ, that in the affairs of human history, traditionally understood as full of sin and chaos between God's original intervention in the glory of the creation and his final intervention in the glory of his final coming, a "new creation" has taken place. The "hymn" that we are about to consider may well have been sung in the Christian community at Philippi. Paul most likely did not invent this hymn. Paul takes the hymn from the prayer life of the Philippians.[17]

---

16 Brendan J. Byrne, *Reckoning with Romans. A Contemporary Reading of Paul's Gospel*, Good News Studies 18 (Wilmington, DE: Michael Glazier, 1986), 224.

17 For a full discussion of this question, see Ralph P. Martin, *Carmen Christi. Philippians ii. 5-11 in Recent Interpretation and in the Setting of Early Christian Worship*, Society for New Testament Studies Monograph Series 4 (Cambridge: Cambridge University Press, 1967), 24-62.

This explains his missionary outreach to the Christians in Philippi: "Let the same mind be in you that was in Christ Jesus" (v. 5). They are to behave as Jesus did, but this is not simply an ethical request, asking them to improve their behavior. To have in mind the same mind as Jesus Christ is another way of stating Paul's command found elsewhere, to "put on Christ." In the Gospels it takes the form of "following Christ." The First Letter of John puts it well when the author asks his readers to put their lives where their words are: "He who *says* he abides in him ought to *walk* in the same way as he walked" (1 John 2:6). The self-emptying of Jesus that lies at the heart of Philippians 2:5-11 should lie at the heart of all who claim to be his followers.

> [T]he transformation is "in Christ," "into Christ," "with Christ," in the "body of Christ," and into the image of Christ, the new creation. If it is true that Christ alone had/has the "native ability" to measure up to God's pattern for humanity, then it is by becoming like Christ that those "in Christ" will satisfy the final inspection. Not by being "in Christ" as a mystical experience or by virtue of an ecclesiastical rite. Not by having righteousness imputed as an "alien righteousness." And certainly not by Pelagian or semi-Pelagian self-effort. But by a progressive transformation into Christ's likeness (2 Cor. 3.18), whose climax and completion is the transformation/resurrection of the body (2 Cor. 4.16–5.5). "Justification" and "new creation" (2 Cor. 5.17; Gal. 6.15) go together.[18]

Paul confronts the problem of division among the Philippians. Immediately prior to his insertion of the hymn into his letter Paul wrote: "Do nothing from selfish ambition or conceit, but in humility

---

[18] James D. G. Dunn, *The New Perspective on Paul*, rev. ed. (Grand Rapids: Eerdmans, 2008), 93-94.

regard others as better than yourselves. Let each of you look not to your own interests, but to the interests of others" (Phil 2:3-4). Once the Philippians encounter the inserted hymn, they become aware that they are having their own words quoted back to them. Paul reminds them of a hymn they sing in praise of Jesus Christ. Their only model can be Jesus, and the hymn that they sing tells his story, but perhaps it is not telling the story of the Philippians. He asks them to put their lives where their words are: "Let the same mind be in you that was in Christ Jesus" (v. 5).

The hymn explains *how* creation began anew in Jesus Christ. This famous hymn unfolds in five stages. The first stage describes Jesus' preparedness to accept humiliation by shedding his pre-existent divine state (vv. 6-7a). The translation of the hymn in the NRSV says that he did not "exploit" his equality with God. Scholars have debated for decades why a rough and almost violent Greek verb (*harpazō*) could be used in a hymn dedicated to Jesus. Its primary dictionary meaning is "to make off with someone's property by attacking or seizing. *Steal, carry off, drag away.*"[19] More than "exploit" is intended, as there is something violent about the verb. He did not grasp the honor of being equal to God rapaciously, violently and arrogantly. Perhaps the verb is well chosen, despite its offensive overtones. It may well be that the Philippians were grasping rapaciously for honors, and that tendency has not come to an end with the Philippians. What must be noticed is that the verb is in the negative! This is what Jesus *did not do*: "he *did not* regard equality with God as something to be exploited." Paul speaks directly to us all. As we seek honors and glory in our achievements, Christ Jesus did exactly the opposite. He lets go of the most wonderful of honors – his oneness with God. His status

---

[19] See Frederick W. Danker, *A Greek-English Lexicon of the New Testament and Other Early Christian Literature* (Chicago: Chicago University Press, 2000), 134, s.v. *harpazō*.

was divine and he let it go; our status is fragile and sinful, but we "grasp onto it jealously."[20] We are again at the heart of our missionary mandate, calling all to such a "conversion," starting with ourselves and our communities.

This leads the hymn into the second stage of Christ's humiliation (vv. 7b-8). Jesus does not simply "let go," but he "empties himself" of all dignity, to take on the situation of a servant and slave. Another remarkable Greek word that has become central to all subsequent thought enters the Christian vocabulary: *kenōsis* (the Greek verb *eskenōsen* is used in the text).[21] This unconditional self-emptying leaves *nothing* of his being in the form of God, *nothing* of his equality with God. A *kenōsis* is a complete self-emptying. The Christ comes into the history of frail human beings as a frail human being: he became as we are. There can be no holding back on this, as Paul and the Philippians did not hold back in their use and acceptance of the word *kenōsis* to speak of Jesus' taking on the human condition with all its joys, pains and limitations. He is not only emptied of all honor, but he takes on the condition of a *doulos*, a Greek word that means either a slave or a servant. In Jesus, it means both!

But a further description of Jesus' humiliation points out that to become human was not enough to effect the new creation. He lowered himself in human eyes to the lowest level possible; he accepted the cruelest and most humiliating death – death on a cross. Israel had already been taught: "Cursed be everyone who hangs on a tree" (Deut 27:26). Unfortunately, we have lost the sense of what death on a cross meant to people living in the Roman era. The cross has been domesticated, reduced to a bauble that one hangs around one's neck or,

---

[20] For a convincing affirmation of the Pauline notion of Christ's pre-existence and its theological importance, see Brendan J. Byrne, "Christ's Pre-Existence in Pauline Soteriology," *Theological Studies* 58 (1997): 308-30.

[21] See Danker, *A Greek-English Lexicon*, 539, s.v. *keneō*.

as Augustine said, from a place of punishment, it became decoration on the emperor's crown. It was the cruelest form of execution that the Romans could devise, generally preceded (as in the case of Jesus) with mockery and the infliction of less mortal insults and suffering. It was reserved only for the lowest of the low, hardened criminals, and for those who dared to challenge the authority of Rome.[22] When Jesus gives his unconditional "yes" to God on the Cross his *kenōsis* and subsequent humiliation are complete.

The hymn has had a downward swing from the Christ equal to God to a crucified slave. The unconditional obedience of Jesus has touched the human story in a "once and for all" fashion, and this has its consequence. Jesus' unconditional "yes" to God is met by an unconditional "yes" from God. The Greek text marks a sharp change of direction, as God enters the story of Jesus, a consequence of Jesus' unconditional acceptance of his will. It states "because of this" (*dio kai*) ... *because of what Jesus did* out of obedience to God and for all of us, he is raised on high by God.[23] God's exaltation of Jesus lies at the center of the hymn (v. 9). The theme of the hymn begins its upward swing with this turning point in the unfolding hymn: God has highly exalted him. The Christ returns to the place he abandoned so that we may have life and hope. The result of God's exaltation of his Son does not lead the Christ to a distant place on the altars on high. It involves all who can claim him as the one who has changed the nature of the relationship between God and humankind because of his unconditional gift of self unto death. As the text makes clear, we are those who will bend the knee and confess Jesus Christ as Lord because of what God has done for us, in and through him.

---

22 On this, see Martin Hengel, *Crucifixion* (London: SCM Press, 1977).
23 The NRSV loses this nuance with its weak "therefore." Jean-François Collange describes the use of *dio kai* as indicating "the gracious sovereign act of God" (*The Epistle of Saint Paul to the Philippians*, trans. A. W. Heathcote [London: Epworth Press, 1979], 105).

The first description of the homage that flows from God's action in the resurrection has a subtle but important nuance. At the name of "Jesus" every knee should bend. The name "Jesus" was the name of a man who lived among us. It was the name of a human being who had shed all his claims to honor, and unconditionally embraced the human condition, even unto death on the Cross. The name of this man, now exalted, must be recognized for what he has done. We are all in his debt, and thus every knee should bend (v. 10). But the exaltation goes further. Not only is the crucified and risen Jesus to be recognized and honored. Jesus Christ must be confessed as "Lord" (*Kyrios*), an expression used in the Greek Bible for the divinity (v. 11).[24] All creation recognizes what Jesus has done, and what God has done in and through him. Every knee bends in recognition of the saving act of God that has taken place through Jesus' obedience unto death in his unconditional "yes" to God and the subsequent (*dio kai*) unconditional "yes" of God's acceptance of that obedience by means of the exaltation that takes place in resurrection.

Jesus Christ is now our Lord and the Lord of all creation: every knee bends and every tongue confesses that the crucified and risen Jesus Christ is Lord. Although not stated in the hymn, the theme of the "new creation" is again central to the Pauline argument. We no longer have to wait for the end of all time for the establishment of God's "right order." It has been made present among us in the new creation in and through the obedient death, resurrection, and universal Lordship of Jesus Christ. We confess that Jesus Christ is Lord; we recognize the glory of God … but only if we are prepared to accept Paul's initial invitation to walk as Jesus walked: "Let the same mind be in you that was in Christ Jesus" (v. 5).

---

[24] See Joseph A. Fitzmyer, "Kyrios," in *Exegetical Dictionary of the New Testament*, ed. Horst Balz and Gerhard Schneider, 3 vols. (Grand Rapids, Eerdmans, 1991), 2:328-31.

MISSION

These famous texts drive us back to consider our missionary mandate. The story of Jesus must be repeated in the story of those who claim to follow him, and its beauty must be portrayed for all who are hearing this message from us for the first time. Our lives can be caught up into the rhythm, scope and ultimate victory of the same divine plan to restore his original creation. But Paul also teaches us something about a missionary method. On two occasions Paul introduces material into his letters that the people receiving them knew well.

In writing to the Corinthians, Paul had heard that there were serious problems with the community celebration of the Lord's Table (1 Cor 11:17-34). Apparently, the wealthy were using these festive meals to show their authority and wealth, gathering at sumptuous tables, and making the Eucharistic meal into a feast that left many of them inebriated. However, at that same meal, they disregarded the poorer members of the community. They were allowed only a marginal participation at the table. As Paul described the situation: "I hear that there are divisions among you. ... In eating each one goes ahead with his own meal and one is hungry and another is drunk. What! Do you not have houses to eat and drink in? Or do you despise the Church of God and humiliate those who have nothing?" (1 Cor 11:19, 21-22). His mind on this matter is quite clear: "When you meet together it is not the Lord's supper that you eat" (v. 20).

To instruct the Corinthians on the true significance of the Eucharistic meal, he reminds them of something they knew very well: the actions and words of Jesus on the night before he died (vv. 23-25). These are *the words and deeds that they recall as they celebrate the Lord's Supper*. Their lives do not match what Jesus did for them, despite the fact that Jesus told them: "Do this in memory of me" (vv. 24, 25). Jesus' loving self-gift for them on the Cross, where his body was broken and his blood was shed, has been forgotten in real life. Nevertheless, in their neglect of one another, they use gestures and words of Jesus that summon them to break their bodies and spill their blood in memory of him.[25]

The same rhetorical practice is found in Philippians 2:5-11, the passage we have just considered at length. In their divisions and arrogant affirmation of their own dignity, Paul reminds the Philippians of something that they pray regularly: their hymn in praise of Jesus' self-emptying and his subsequent exaltation by God. If they are to participate in the new creation, they are to let go of their selfish arrogance, so caught up in the arrogance left in human history by the sin of Adam, and become imitators of Jesus Christ. In this way their lives will proclaim what God has done for us in and through Jesus, until he comes again. This missionary message, in all its richness, must be preached "in season and out of season" (2 Tim 4:2).

CONCLUSION

Paul has developed, at the dawn of Christianity, rich expressions: "with Christ," "life in Christ," and "to put on Christ." Several of them run together in Paul's famous words to the Galatians, "I have been crucified with Christ. It no longer I who live, but Christ who lives in me; and the life I now live in the flesh I live by faith in the Son of God, who loved me and gave himself for me" (Gal 2:20). Much can be gleaned from these powerful images, and the many parallel passages from across the Pauline writings. They form part of the contemporary missionary invitation to reach out *ad Gentes*, and the call of the New Evangelization to renew the Christianity of a post-Christian era. Behind these expressions lies the Pauline missionary invitation to

---

[25] See Francis J. Moloney, *A Body Broken for a Broken People. Divorce, Remarriage, and the Eucharist*, 3rd ed. (Mulgrave, VIC: John Garratt, 2015), 53-57.

become part of the new creation. Through the death and resurrection of his obedient Son, Jesus Christ, God has entered the human story, once dominated by chaos and sin (see Rom 1:18–3:20). Since the time of Moses, Israel has been protected but not saved by the Law (see Rom 5:14, and especially 7:7-25). The creative action of God, present at the beginning of all time, and expected again at the end of all time, has now become available within the span of human history (see Gal 6:15; 2 Cor 5:17). The death and resurrection of the obedient Jesus Christ have reversed the universal sin and death that flowed from the actions of the disobedient Adam. "Anyone in Christ is a new creation. The old has passed away; behold the new has come" (2 Cor 5:17). We have privileged access to God's glory in a way that was expected only at the end of time. Using theological language, we can say that for Paul, believers are an "eschatological people of God." A missionary is asked to invite everyone to become part of that people of God.

However, as we saw in our reflection on the Adam-Christ relationship, we live in a time and a situation of tension: both sin and grace abound. The story of Adam and the story of Christ co-exist; they run parallel in our world, our society and our own lives (see Rom 5:12-21). Paul believes, of course, that where sin abounds, grace super-abounds, but one must be prepared to put on Christ in order to enter the new creation. Christian life is an attempt to live as Jesus lived, to obey as Jesus obeyed, to imitate him in every way, to be crucified with Christ, to live a life in the flesh that manifests that we believe in Jesus Christ as Son and Savior. It is for this reason that Paul can remind us of the great rule of life, "Faith, hope and love abide, these three: but the greatest of these is love" (1 Cor 13:13. See also 1 Thess 4:9-12; Gal 5:13-15; Rom 13:8-10; Phlm 15-20).[26]

---

26 The primacy of the law of love, of course, is something that Paul shares with Jesus, and with the rest of the New Testament and the early Church. See Victor P. Furnish, *The Love Command in the New Testament* (London: SCM Press, 1973).

But as we have seen in our reflections upon Romans, Philippians, and 1 Corinthians, even Christian communities where Paul had worked tirelessly to proclaim his Gospel of a new creation, were not living as they preached and prayed (see 1 Cor 11:17-34; Phil 2:4-11). Paul was quick to remind them that in order to belong to the new creation, they had to put their lives where their words were. The message of the new creation is not only something we preach to *others*. Paul recalled the story of Jesus for people who already claimed to know it well. But he asks them to live as he did, in memory of him. In order to be effective missionaries of the new creation, where the old had passed away, and where all things were new, to experience "life in Christ," we must live as Jesus lived.

Called to be missionaries within the context of the new creation generated by the death and resurrection of Jesus Christ, we must never forget the dignity that is ours. As Paul angrily warns the Galatians, "For freedom Christ has set us free; stand fast therefore, and do not submit again to the yoke of slavery" (Gal 5:1). But this calls for courage. Each of us experiences the obvious presence of the Adam-story and its slaveries that surround us, and the never-ending challenge to live as Christ lived and loved. In the Western world, such a lifestyle is ridiculed.

Indeed, a missionary activity proclaiming the life-giving message of the joy and freedom of the new creation established by the death and resurrection of Jesus can be judged as a system based on a fairy tale, an unacceptable invasion of the minds, hearts and the imagination of a highly secularized culture. We live in perplexing and challenging times, and we sometimes wonder why things are the way they are, and why there is so much misunderstanding and lack of trust and confidence in what we do and why we do it.

Toward the end of the Letter to the Romans, in chapters 9-11, Paul agonizes over the fact that the bulk of Israel had rejected Jesus as the Christ, while many Gentiles had accepted him. He opens his reflection asking: "What shall we say then? That Gentiles who did not pursue righteousness have attained it, that is, righteousness through faith; but that Israel who pursued the righteousness which is based on Law did not succeed in fulfilling that law" (Rom 9:30-31). Toward the close of his pondering he further asks, "Has God rejected his people?" and responds, "By no means! I myself am an Israelite, a descendant of Abraham, a member of the tribe of Benjamin" (Rom 11:1). It is not possible that God will not maintain his promises, but – despite Paul's bold articulation of his belief in God's ultimate designs for Israel – he can find no answer to the problem he has raised so acutely. Paul's mission to his own people has failed.

As we puzzle over the sometimes hostile and increasingly mobile environment within which we exercise our missionary ministry, Paul's writing can again be instructive. He places all his trust in the God and Father of Jesus Christ. As he closes his perplexed questioning of his failed mission among his own people, he cries out:

> O the depths of the riches and the wisdom and
> the knowledge of God!
>
> How unsearchable are his judgments and how
> inscrutable his ways!
>
> For who has known the mind of the Lord, or
> who has been his counselor?
>
> Or who has given a gift to him that he might be
> repaid?
>
> For from him and through him and to him are
> all things.
>
> To him be glory forever. Amen. (Rom 11:33-36)

2

THE GOSPEL OF MARK

The Twelve, Mission, and Failure: "He is going before you into Galilee" (Mark 16:7)

The best of "Christian achievers" are those who realistically accept the brokenness present in their own lives, and who in turn offer a fragile hand to those who, often through no fault of their own, are forced to the margins of society. Fascinatingly, this is one of the features of the characterization of the disciples of Jesus in the Gospel of Mark.[1] There are many indications that Jesus pursues a relentless missionary journey, from his telling his disciples that he must move on, away from Capernaum, "for that is what I came out to do" (Mark 1:38) at the beginning of his ministry until three women find an empty tomb.

---

1   The names "Mark," "Matthew," "Luke," and "John" were added to the Gospel manuscripts late in the second Christian century. We cannot be sure of the exact names and background of the historical authors, but I will use the traditional names, for ease of reference, and out of respect for the tradition. On the disciples in Mark, among many studies, see Francis J. Moloney, *Mark: Storyteller, Interpreter, Evangelist* (Peabody, MA: Hendrickson, 2004), 164-93.

His journey to Jerusalem, the Cross and resurrection is dominated by verbs of motion, regularly linked with the adverb "immediately" (Greek: *euthus*. See 1:14, 16, 19, 21, 29, 32, 39, 40; 2:1, 13, 23; 3:1, 7, 13, etc.).

However, there are only three places in the Gospel where the theme of mission is explicitly associated with the disciples. The first two are closely related: Jesus' appointment of the disciples to accompany him in his mission in Mark 3:13-19, and their being sent out on mission in 6:6b-30. The third explicit association of the disciples with the mission of Jesus is more subtle: the message that he is going before them into Galilee, given to the women by the young man at the empty tomb (16:7. See 14:28). Even though we are mainly concerned with those three passages, properly to understand the full extent of Mark's missionary message, we must look at the whole canvas of Mark's narrative. Each passage has its own context in the wider story, and a biblical text must be interpreted within its context.[2]

THE GOSPEL STORY

The Gospel of Mark traces the God-directed passing of time, systematically articulated in the larger blocks of material and the smaller episodes that unfold within them, according to a logic that leads inevitably toward the Cross. The audience is led further into a story whose ending is known, yet is surprised on the way – and at the end. The plot is shot through with hints that look forward to the end of the story. The Gospel of Mark is unique among the Gospels

---

2   As I regularly say to my students: "Text without context is pretext." One of the difficulties in our Sunday encounters with the Word of God in the Liturgy is that we are unable to understand the single passages that are proclaimed within their larger context of their role in the story as a whole. For an earlier version of this chapter, see Francis J. Moloney, "Mark 6:6b-30: The Twelve, Mission, and Failure," in *Gospel Interpretation and Christian Life*, Scholars Collection 3 (Adelaide: ATF Theology, 2017), 15-45.

because, unlike most narratives (including Matthew, Luke and John), the crises that emerge during the narrative are not resolved through a *dénouement* at the end of the story (see Mark 16:1-8). Much is resolved, but a further crisis emerges which cannot be resolved by the story itself. The women are given a commission to announce the Easter message to the disciples, and to instruct them on Jesus' future encounter with them in Galilee. But they are so frightened, they say nothing to anyone (see 16:6-8). This suggests that the crisis might be resolved in the lives of the people reading and hearing the story.[3]

In a good story the reader is told enough to be made curious, without ever being given all the answers. Narrative texts keep promising the great prize of understanding – later.[4] The "later" of the Gospel of Mark, I suggest, is the "now" of the Christian reader. If this is true, then the single parts of the story, in our case Mark 3:13-19, 6:6a-30, and 16:1-8 might helpfully be read in the light of the "now" of a Christian audience as we focus upon the call to a Christian mission at the first decades of the third millennium.

As the plot of the Gospel of Mark unfolds there are signs within the narrative that indicate a change of direction to the audience. They can be called "textual markers." These textual markers show that the author is "up to something." There are six major moments when the reader meets significant turning points in the story. The "good news" begins (1:1), Jesus initiates his ministry in Galilee (1:14-15), he announces his forthcoming death and resurrection for the first time (8:31), he enters Jerusalem (11:1-11), a decision is made that Jesus must be arrested and killed (14:1-2), and women discover an empty

---

[3] Mark is a storyteller of great subtlety. Among many, see Kelly R. Iverson and Christopher W. Skinner, eds., *Mark as Story. Retrospect and Prospect*, Society for Biblical Literature Resources for Biblical Study 65 (Altanta: Society for Biblical Literature, 2011).

[4] See Shlomith Rimmon-Kenan, *Narrative Fiction. Contemporary Poetics*, New Accents (London: Methuen, 1983), 125.

tomb (16:1-4). Although it may come as a surprise to those who are meeting Gospel studies for the first time, this story line was invented by the Evangelist Mark, and its appearance in the first early Christian "Gospel" was intentionally a theological statement. *Whatever the first readers knew of the life-story of Jesus of Nazareth was subverted by the Markan story. The Markan plot of Jesus' presence in Galilee, his journey to Jerusalem, the Cross, the resurrection and the silence of the women was not familiar to the early Christian world.* Such a "plot" saw the light of day *for the first time* when Mark invented it. It was accepted by Matthew and Luke as the basic story line for their accounts of Jesus' life, death, and resurrection. This *radical newness* of the Markan story for its first audiences must be kept in mind.[5] It is an original way of telling the story of Jesus. The Gospel of John, perhaps more closely reflecting the sequence of events in the life of Jesus, did not follow Mark in this.[6]

One can trace the following temporal and geographical strategies.

1. Mark 1:1-13 serves as a prologue to the Gospel providing the reader with a great deal of information about God's beloved Son.

2. Through Mark 1:14–8:30 the words and deeds of Jesus' ministry increasingly force the question: who is this man (see 1:27, 45; 2:12; 3:22; 4:41; 5:20; 6:2-3, 48-50; 7:37)? Some accept him, some do not care, and many oppose him. The question behind this first half of the story is: can he be the Messiah? In 8:29 Peter, in the name of the disciples, resolves the problem by

---

[5] See the important essay by Eduard Schweizer, first published in 1964: "Mark's Theological Achievement," in William Telford, ed., *The Interpretation of Mark*, Issues in Religion and Theology 7 (Philadelphia: Fortress, 1985), 42-63.

[6] See Francis J. Moloney, "The Fourth Gospel and the Jesus of History," *New Testament Studies* 45 (1999): 42-58.

confessing: "You are the Messiah." The guessing has come to an end, even though Peter may not have correctly understood what he confessed. Jesus warns the disciples not to talk about it (v. 30).

3. Mark 8:31–10:52 reports Jesus' journey to Jerusalem, largely focused upon Jesus' teaching of his oncoming death and resurrection (8:31; 9:31; 10:32-34) and his instruction of increasingly frightened disciples.

4. He enters Jerusalem (11:1-11), brings all Temple practice to an end (11:12-24), encounters and silences Israel's religious authorities (11:27–12:44), and prophesies the end of the Holy City and the world (13:1-37).

5. Jesus enters his passion and death (14:1–15:47). If 1:14–8:30 made it clear that Jesus is the Messiah (8:29) yet suggesting that this may not be the whole truth (8:30), the second half of the Gospel explains further. Jesus is a suffering Messiah, the Son of Man (8:31; 9:31; 10:32-33). In 15:37 a Roman centurion confesses: "Truly this man was God's Son!" The suffering Son of Man is truly the Son of God.

6. Many questions raised by the story remain unresolved. The disciples have fled (see 14:50) and Jesus has cried out: "My God, my God, why have you forsaken me?" (15:34). Jesus' question is resolved in the concluding story of women visiting an empty tomb. In 16:1-8 the reader learns that God has not forsaken his Son. He has been raised (see 16:6). But the solution to the problem of failing disciples lies in the future. They are to go into Galilee, there they will see him (v. 7. See

14:28). The women, frightened by what they have seen and heard, flee and say nothing to anyone (v. 8).[7]

Within this simple but skillfully planned overall story of the life, death, and resurrection of Jesus, two of the passages that concern the mission of the disciples (3:13-19 and 6:6b-30) are found in the ministry in Galilee, reported in 1:14–8:30. Once again, in order properly to grasp the full possibilities of our mission passages, we need to look even more closely at this broader context.

MARK 1:14–8:30

The first half of the story wonders whether Jesus is the Messiah. The second half portrays him as the Messiah who is the suffering Son of Man, the crucified Son of God. The two "halves" of the plot, however, overlap. Peter's confession of faith in Mark 8:29 and Jesus' response in v. 30 might mark the closure of the Galilean ministry, but a theme of "blindness" has emerged in 8:22-26 in the strange story of a blind man at Bethsaida who has his sight restored in stages. This theme will be resumed in 10:46-52 where a further story of a man coming to sight is reported: the story of blind Bartimaeus. Between these two miracle stories, where blind men are cured, Jesus speaks of the oncoming death and resurrection of the Son of Man (see 8:31; 9:31; 10:32-35) and instructs increasingly frightened disciples who will not or cannot understand what it means to follow Jesus (see 8:32-33; 9:33-37; 10:36-45). They too suffer from blindness. As Jesus asks them in 8:18: "Do you have eyes and fail to see?"

---

[7] On the suggestion that the original ending to the Gospel of Mark, reporting appearances of the risen Christ, was lost, see below, p. 50, n. 22.

Mark 1:14–8:30 establishes relationships, and raises questions concerning the person of Jesus. The Gospel of Mark is not only about Jesus, Son of God and Christ. It is equally about the challenge of "following" him to Jerusalem – and beyond (see 1:16-20; 2:15-17). On three occasions across Mark 1:1–8:30 the narrator makes a general statement (generally called a "summary") about Jesus' ministry, which introduces a series of events illustrating that activity (see 1:14-15; 3:7-12; 6:6a). There are, of course, other similar general statements or summaries of Jesus' ministry in the Gospel (see, for example, 1:39, 45b; 4:33-34; 6:53-56; 9:30-31; 10:1). What is unique about these three, however, is that each of them is immediately followed by material that deals with disciples and discipleship (1:16-20; 3:13-19; 6:6b-13). The three summaries each begin a part of the story that leads directly into passages which deal with disciples, and close with decisions made either for or against Jesus.

1. In 1:14-15 we read a summary of the ministry of Jesus: "Now after John was arrested, Jesus came to Galilee, proclaiming the good news of God, and saying, 'The time is fulfilled and the kingdom of God has come near, repent and believe in the good news.'" This summary is immediately followed by the account of the vocation of the first disciples (1:16-20). Jesus then exercises his ministry in Galilee, chiefly at Capernaum (1:21–3:6), until representatives of the Jewish people, the political leaders and the religious authorities, respond to him: "The Pharisees went out and immediately conspired with the Herodians against him, how to destroy him" (3:6).

2. In 3:7-12 we find a lengthy general statement about Jesus' Galilean ministry. It concludes with the following summary: "He had cured many so that all

who had diseases pressed upon him to touch him. Whenever the unclean spirits saw him, they fell down before him and shouted, 'You are the Son of God!' But he sternly ordered them not to make him known" (3:10-12). This summary leads into the account of Jesus' institution of the Twelve (3:13-19). But the wonder of Jesus' ministry meets opposition from his family and from Israel (3:20-35). He teaches them through parables (4:1-34) and a stunning series of miracles (4:35–5:43). Returning to his hometown, his own people reject him: "Is not this the carpenter, the son of Mary and brother of James and Joses and Judas and Simon, and are not his sisters here with us?' And they took offense at him" (6:3). Jesus was "amazed at their unbelief" (6:6a).

3. Immediately following Jesus' rejection in his hometown, we find another brief general summary about his ministry in Galilee: "Then he went about among the villages teaching" (6:6b). This is immediately followed by Jesus' sending out the Twelve on a mission which parallels his own (6:6b-13). The narrative is now marked by increasing hostility between Jesus and the Jews (see 7:1-23), and a deeper involvement of his disciples, his new family, with his ministry (see 6:7-13, 30-44; 8:1-10). It draws to a close as the question which has been lurking behind the narrative from 1:14 is broached by two questions asked by Jesus: "Who do people say that I am?" (8:27), and "Who do you say that I am?" (v. 28). Peter responds: "You are the Messiah" (v. 29). There is a sense in which Peter is correct, but the report of Jesus' warning to the disciples

("them") sounds a warning bell, and opens the door to the second part of the Gospel: "He charged them to tell no one about him" (8:30). As we have already suggested, the second half of the Gospel will show that Peter - and all the disciples - still have a long way to go.

Although we will not focus upon the vocation of the disciples in 1:16-20 at length, their mission is already indicated in this first moment of interaction between Jesus and his disciples. They are to "follow" Jesus and become fishers of people (see vv. 17, 18, 20). The use of the Greek verb "to follow" (*akoloutheō*) is open to two meanings. In the first place, it can have the meaning of committing oneself to the same dreams and ideals as Jesus, as one could be a follower of any great hero (e.g., Mahatma Gandi). But it also means "to walk behind," to join someone in a journey where he or she leads the way. The "follower" does not know the path, nor the end point of the journey, but walks with trust, steadily following the steps of the leader. These first vocation stories (1:16-20) establish a significant association between the disciples and his eventual journey to Jerusalem. But at this stage of Mark's story, this association does not contain a participation in his mission. Jesus' interaction with his disciples that open the second and the third section of the story of the Galilean ministry, 3:13-19 and 6:6b-30 are explicitly missionary.

MARK 3:13-19

A major Markan contribution to the tradition on the sending out of the missionaries is the indication of their sharing in the mission of Jesus. This is particularly clear in the commissioning of the Twelve in 3:14-15. This passage is immediately preceded by the summary of the increasing intensity of Jesus' ministry in the summary of 3:7-12.

The disciples have been called in 1:16-20, and they have been at Jesus' side from that time on. However, the Twelve are called into a deeper relationship with Jesus in 3:13-14, as crowds come to him and his ministry expands. Initially calling a larger group of disciples, "those whom he wanted" (v. 13), he then institutes the Twelve. He appoints them *to be with him* (v. 14. Greek: *einai met'autou*). The expression does not simply mean to "accompany" Jesus in some way. It is a more intimate association of the Twelve "with Jesus" that authorizes them to do what, up to this point in the story, only Jesus has done. Jesus is the one who was sent out to preach (see 1:14-15, 27, 38-39; 2:2, 13) and to have authority over demons (see 1:21-28, 32-34, 39; 3:11-12). The Twelve are promised a share in this mission in 3:14-15. The most significant element, however, in the Twelve's sharing in the mission of Jesus is that they "be with him … so that they might …" (3:14-15). Grammatically (and theologically) their being sent out to preach, and their having authority over demons in 3:14b-15, depends upon their *being with him* in v. 14a.

One could state the Markan affirmation negatively as follows: associated with Jesus, the Twelve have authority to preach and cast out demons, but separated from Jesus, all such authority will cease. It would no longer have its source in the relationship initiated and established by Jesus. Jesus says this in John 15:5: "Without me you can do nothing." *He* appointed the Twelve (3:14). What they are to do in mission depends entirely upon their never-failing union *with Jesus*. The initiative of Jesus continues in the naming of the disciples that follows. He gives an extra name to the first three of the Twelve mentioned: Simon is given the name "Peter" (v. 16), and James and John are given the name "Boanerges, that is, sons of thunder" (v. 17). In the biblical tradition, to name someone or something makes them especially associated with you. The best-known examples are Adam's naming of all the animals (Gen 3:19), and of his partner Eve as "woman" (Gen 2:23). As the Gospel unfolds, Peter, James, and John play a more intimate role in Jesus' ministry (see 5:37 [raising Jairus' daughter]; 9:2 [Transfiguration]; 14:33 [Gethsemane]) because they belong to Jesus in a special way.

The names of the Twelve are provided in vv. 16-18. However, special attention is given to the twelfth name: Judas Iscariot. Mark describes Judas as "the one who betrayed him" (v. 19). This is an adequate translation of the Greek (*hos kai paredōken auton*), but there is a deeper meaning in the verb rendered "betrayed." The primary meaning of the Greek verb *paradidōmi* is "to hand over" in both a positive (e.g., "entrust something to someone") or a negative sense (e.g., "to give up or hand over a person").[8] For the audience of the Gospel of Mark, the latter meaning is clearly understood in the light of what they know about Judas' betrayal of Jesus. In this way, Judas rejects what he was offered in v. 14. As this passage *begins*, Judas is appointed to an intimate union with Jesus and his mission, called to be "with him." As the report of the appointment of the Twelve *ends* the audience is reminded that Judas deliberately separated himself from Jesus, he "handed him over." This literary pattern is called an "inclusion": a link is made between what is essential for a missionary discipleship as the passage opens (v. 14: to be with Jesus), and the reason for total failure as it closes (v. 19: to hand him over). Our reading of 3:13-19 provides a key to the second explicit missionary passage, one of the most puzzling sequences in Mark's Gospel: 6:6b-30.

MARK 6:6b-30

One of the features of Markan style is the use of so-called "sandwich" constructions. Another term for this literary technique is "intercalation." Mark regularly begins a narrative, breaks into it with another narrative, and closes the passage by returning to the story

---

[8] See Danker, ed., *A Greek-English Lexicon*, 761-62, s.v. *paradidōmi*, §1ab.

he had begun earlier. Two of these "sandwich" constructions are well known. Earlier in the story the reader finds the intercalation of the curing of the woman with the flow of blood set between Jairus' request that Jesus cure his daughter, and Jesus' coming to Jairus' home and raising the young woman (5:21-24a [Jesus and Jairus], 24b-34 [Jesus and the woman], 35-43 [Jesus raises Jairus' daughter]). Later, after his arrival in Jerusalem for the first and only time (11:1-11), as Jesus walks with his disciples from Bethany to Jerusalem, he curses a fig tree, brings all activity in the Temple to a stand-still, and the next day the disciples notice the dead fig tree (11:12-14 [Jesus curses the fig tree], 15-19 [all Temple activity is brought to an end], 20-21 [the fig tree has withered]). There are several other intercalations, or sandwich constructions in the Gospel of Mark (see, for example, 3:20-35; 4:1-32; 6:21-35; 14:17-31; 14:53-72).

The expression "sandwich" is opportune, as very frequently in these simple but effective literary structures, the passage "in the middle" has a determining influence on the meaning of the passage. In the traditional Anglo-Saxon understanding of the expression, to indicate which kind of "sandwich" one is ordering, one asks – for example – for a "ham and cheese sandwich."[9] The ham and cheese are placed between two slices of bread, that form a "frame" for the contents that give the sandwich its name. A Markan literary sandwich is created by Mark in 6:6b-30. An audience is aware that the material "in the middle" of the sandwich is crucial for an interpretation of the passage as a whole.

The summary statement of 6:6b follows hard upon the rejection of Jesus in his hometown (6:1-6a). He leaves Nazareth, teaching in

---

9   In the United States a "sandwich" is more complex. It does not catch the nature of the Markan literary structure. Normally (things can vary from region to region), it is a large plate full of a number of components, generally including chips (or "fries") most likely with extra sauces, etc., "on the side."

other villages, "And he called to him the Twelve, and began to send them out two by two" (v. 7a). The remainder of v. 7 recalls the earlier association of the Twelve with Jesus in 3:13-14, and in vv. 8-9 the narrator continues to report explicit instructions on what they are to take on the mission. Vv. 10-11 are marked by a change from the narrator's report to the direct speech of Jesus. He gives instructions on how they are to behave in a concrete missionary situation. Vv. 12-13 then reports the success of those who were sent out in v. 7. They scatter to do the things that Jesus has done (6:12b-13).

Without any introduction, while the Twelve are on their mission, the section on the death of the Baptist follows (vv. 14-29). This passage appears "in the middle" of the literary sandwich.

Mark returns to his missionaries in v. 30. The "going out" of the Twelve is reversed as the narrator tells the reader that they "gathered around Jesus." Indeed, more than a simple return to the geographical place which they had left earlier is implied by the verb "to gather around" (*sunagontai*). They do not simply return, but they come back to be with Jesus again (see 3:14). Jesus' action of "sending out" in v. 7a is recalled as those who return are described as the "sent ones." There is no need to associate the use of the noun "the sent ones" in v. 30 with the technical title "the apostles," an expression never found in this sense in the Gospel of Mark. The Twelve are called "those sent out" in v. 30 because they were the ones whom Jesus began to "send out" in v. 7a.

Mark has created the following sandwich construction:

vv. 6b-13: The association of the disciples with the mission of Jesus, as they are "sent out." They are scattered as they go, two by two, to their successful missionary activity.

vv. 14-29: The death of John the Baptist.

v. 30: The return of those "sent out" to make their report to Jesus. They "gather" and tell Jesus what they have said and done.

An awareness of Mark's widespread use of these sandwich constructions (or intercalations) warns the audience that the account of the death of John the Baptist (vv. 14-29) must play a major role in the interpretation of 6:6b-30.[10]

Mark 6:6b-13

Associating the disciples with Jesus' mission of preaching in v. 6b, vv. 7-13 is made up of three parts: vv. 7-9: the giving of authority and the external signs of the missionary are reported; vv. 10-11: Jesus' instruction on the behavior of the missionaries in the field; vv. 12-13: The storyteller reports the success of the mission of the Twelve.

(a) Mark 6:7-9

Scholars regularly point to the instructions – no bread, no bag, no money, and only one tunic - as a deliberate attempt on the part of the early Christian missionaries to separate themselves from the wandering Cynic preachers who were allowed such trappings. Crucial, however, for Mark is Jesus' giving authority to the Twelve over the unclean spirits (v. 7). Such authority, up to this point of the narrative, belonged only to Jesus (see 1:27). It was earlier promised to the Twelve, appointed to be with him (3:14-15). The promise now becomes reality as the disciples are formally given a share in Jesus' authority over the demons.

Only in Mark are the Twelve *permitted* to take a staff and to wear sandals (6:8-9. Contrast Matt 10:10; Luke 10:4). A feature of Mark's

---

10 See James R. Edwards, "Marcan Sandwiches: The Significance of Interpolations in Marcan Narratives," *Novum Testamentum* 31 (1989): 193-216.

Gospel is the presentation of Jesus as a preacher and a miracle worker who is forever on a journey, driven by the divine urgency which marks this charismatic wanderer (see 1:9, 14, 16, 19, 21, 29, 35; 2:1, 13, 23; 3:1, 7, etc.). The staff and the sandals are symbols of this lifestyle, and the disciples, devoid of all necessities, are permitted to join Jesus in his missionary journey. They are resourced by their dependence upon Jesus (3:13-14), by their being "followers" of Jesus (1:16-20), joining him in his response to a God-directed journey. Their taking nothing else is a further sign: they depend totally upon him. "Messengers are not to be believed if they rely upon their own resources (material or spiritual) rather than on the One whom they proclaim."[11]

Disciples have been chosen by Jesus (see 1:16-20; 2:13-14; 3:13) and from among them, Jesus has "instituted" the Twelve (3:14). The disciples and thus also the Twelve are followers of Jesus (1:16-20; 2:13-14). They are intimately associated with him (3:14) and it is from this intimate association that their mission flows (3:14b-15). The Twelve are missionaries of Jesus only in so far as they respond to the initiative of Jesus, remain with him, recognize that their authority to preach and cast out demons is from him. They are always "followers" of Jesus, and never self-reliant agents.

(b) Mark 6:10-11

The instructions on the behavior of the missionaries in any given situation reflect the experience of the earliest missionary activity of the Christian communities. The literary form changes, from the report of vv. 7-9 into the direct speech of vv. 10-11. Mark is using a tradition that came to him from the setting of early Christian missionary practice. All three Synoptic Gospels, when they come to deal with the question of mission, report these words of Jesus to establish principles that

---

[11] Eduard Schweizer, *The Good News According to Mark*, trans. Donald H. Madvig (London: SPCK, 1971), 130.

might guide the wandering missionaries. The same advice is given in other early Christian documents, like the *Didache* 11.1-2: a warning and a recognition of the importance of the task of the missionary preaching the kingdom of God.[12]

Missionaries were to stay in the first house that offered them accommodation. To arrive in a village, begin preaching the Gospel, but then be seen to move from house to house – perhaps in pursuit of better lodgings or more congenial company – would make a lie of the Gospel the missionary was preaching. Jesus warns: "When you enter a house, stay there until you leave the place" (v. 10. See also *Didache* 11:3-6). It is on Jesus' authority that missioners are now warned that they must live the Gospel they claim to preach. This is an early Christian recommendation to put one's life where one's words are.

Jesus' second recommendation is linked to a practice reported in later Jewish literature. Shaking off the dust from the feet comes from the belief that Israel was God's "holy land." Returning from the impure lands which surrounded Israel, travelers would shake the dust from their feet. This gesture indicated the impurity and godlessness of the land they had just left, and the holiness of the land they were entering.[13]

In the early Christian mission this gesture becomes a sign of judgment. The place that did not receive the missionary, or would not hear the proclamation of the Gospel, was to be judged as "godless" by means of a symbolic shaking of the dust from the feet of the missionary. Symbolically, they cannot claim to belong to God's chosen people, now described as the reigning presence of God as King. This was to

---

12 For the text of the *Didache*, see Michael W. Holmes, *The Apostolic Fathers. Greek Texts and English Translations*, 3rd ed. (Grand Rapids: Baker Academic, 2007). For the above reference, see p. 363.

13 For this practice in later rabbinic writings, see the Mishnah, *Oholoth* 2.3; *Tohoroth* 4.5; and the Babylonian Talmud, *Shabbath* 15b.

be a sign, a witness (v. 11), against all who rejected the opportunity offered by the Christian missionary. The missionaries who put their lives where their words are, proclaim the Gospel in both word and deed (v. 10). They thus had authority to indicate to that place which rejected the missionary and the Gospel message that it had brought judgment upon itself (v. 11). The missionary, "witness" to the message, is not rejected, as they have authority as *emissaries of Jesus* (see 1:16-20; 2:13-17; 3:13). Missionaries have authority because of their "being with him" (3:14). It is not the missionary who is rejected, but the possibility of entering into the reigning presence of God as King.

(c) Mark 6:12-13

What Jesus said *would* happen, *does* happen. This is not surprising. However, Mark reports activities on the part of the missionaries that were not part of the commission of v. 7. There they were given authority over the unclean spirits. However, in vv. 12-13a, as well as casting out demons, they also preach conversion. They "preach that people should convert." This preaching of conversion associates them even more profoundly with the mission of Jesus. As the Gospel opened, Jesus burst upon the scene and placed his ministry under the rubric of preaching conversion: "The time is fulfilled, and the kingdom of God has come near, repent and believe in the Gospel" (1:15).

The healing of the sick is a further association of the missionary activity of the Twelve with the ministry of Jesus up to this point in the narrative (see 1:29-31, 34, 40-45; 2:1-12; 3:1-6, 10; 5:25-34; 6:5). The link between the successful mission of the disciples and their healing of the sick (v. 13), reported in such close literary proximity to Jesus' failed mission in his own town (6:1-6a), where all he could do was heal some of the sick (6:5), is ironic. The Twelve take over and expand the mission of Jesus. The practice of anointing the sick with oil was widespread in the Hellenistic world, and by the time of the writing of the Gospel of Mark had probably become part of Christian practice (see especially Luke 10:34; James 5:14).[14]

In some ways the Twelve are more successful than Jesus had been in the immediately previous scene: Jesus in his hometown (6:1-6a). Earlier parts of the narrative continue to impact upon the audience. Disciples have been chosen by Jesus (see 1:16-20; 2:13-14; 3:13) and from among them, Jesus has further "instituted" the Twelve (3:14). The disciples, and thus also the Twelve, are to be followers of Jesus (1:16-20; 2:13-14). They are intimately associated with him (3:14) and it is from this intimate association that their mission flows (3:14b-15). Like Jesus, they go out, preach conversion (v. 12; 1:14-15), drive out demons and heal the sick (v. 13; 6:5). *The Twelve are missionaries of Jesus only in so far as they respond to the initiative of Jesus, remain with him, recognize that their authority to preach conversion, to cast out demons and to heal the sick is from him. They must be "followers" of Jesus, and never self-reliant agents. Without him, they can do nothing* (see 3:14-15. See also John 15:5).

Mark 6:14-29

Professor Morna Hooker, in her outstanding commentary on the Gospel of Mark, represents majority opinion on the location of the episode of the execution of John the Baptist in the Gospel:

> Between the account of the sending out of the Twelve and that of their return, Mark inserts an account of Herod's reaction to the rumours about Jesus, together with the story of his beheading of John the Baptist.[15] There seems no logical connection between the two themes, but the

---

[14] For a full discussion of this issue, see Luke T. Johnson, *The Letter of James*, Anchor Bible 37a (New York: Doubleday, 1995), 330-32.

[15] The Herod in question is Herod Antipas, who was the tetrarch over Galilee and Perea (east of the Jordan) from 4 BCE till 39 CE.

somewhat artificial insertion provides an interlude for the disciples to complete their mission.[16]

This is not an appropriate understanding of the Markan story. The framing of vv. 14-29 by vv. 6b-13 and v. 30 provide a very "logical sequence to the two themes." There are two parts to the report on the death of the Baptist. Herod's concerns over Jesus are reported in vv. 14-16. This passage is christological, but Herod entwines the figure of John the Baptist in his assessment of Jesus. The first reason given for the increasing fame of Jesus is the suggestion on the part of "some" that John the Baptist has been raised from the dead (v. 14). The resurrection of John the Baptist may point to an expected eschatological prophet. This would indicate that Jesus, John the Baptist *redivivus* (come back to life) would thus be the prophet of the end-time, possessing great powers (v. 14).

Perhaps there is no need to make such a dramatic link between John the Baptist and Jesus. As Hooker remarks, "It is not clear what is meant by the suggestion that John the Baptizer has been raised from the dead; if such a rumor ever circulated, then the idea of an individual being raised was not incredible in popular imagination."[17] The opinion expressed in v. 14 may be as simple as that. Thus it may not be very different from the opinion of "others" who suggest that Jesus is one or other of the several expected prophetic forerunners to the messianic era: Elijah (see Mal 4:5-6), or one of the prophets from of old (with possible links to Deut 18:18), found in v. 15. A Christian audience knows that all such suggestions miss the point, but the question, "who is Jesus" continues to be raised by the characters in the story.[18]

---

16 Morna D. Hooker, *The Gospel According to Saint Mark*, Black's New Testament Commentaries (London: A. & C. Black, 1991), 158.
17 Hooker, *Saint Mark*, 159.
18 The audience is aware of who Jesus is from the prologue to the Gospel (1:1-13), but the characters in the story are not. See Moloney, *Mark: Storyteller*, 59-63.

Herod takes the former option. He decides that Jesus must be the risen John the Baptist, whom he beheaded (v. 16). These words from Herod ("John, whom I beheaded") allow Mark to pick up the tale of John's martyrdom, reporting it in a lengthy flashback in vv. 17-29. For the audience, the issue has been raised of the relationship between John the Baptist and Jesus, and with it the awareness that as the Baptist went to death, so also must Jesus. It is helpful to be aware that for the Jewish historian Josephus (37-100 CE), Herod killed the Baptist because he was afraid of a rebellion by the people (*Antiquities* 18.116-119).[19] This enables us to see Mark's theological focus more clearly.[20] The christological issues raised in vv. 14-16 lie hidden underneath the folkloric narrative of vv. 17-29. For Mark, John the Baptist is put to death by a ruler who recognized that he was "a righteous and holy man" (v. 20. See also v. 26), but who succumbed to public pressure (see vv. 22-26). The Baptist would not give in weakly to pressure, even from one who recognized his virtues. He stood by his God-given task, preaching repentance and forgiveness of sins (see 1:4). For Mark, John's judgment of Herod's marriage is a public call that sinfulness be recognized (see 6:17-19).

Jesus was also executed by a ruler who recognized his goodness (see 15:9-10, 12, 14), but who succumbed to public pressure (see 15:10, 14-15). Jesus does not give in to such pressures, not even to save

---

19 Josephus wrote major works on the *Jewish War* and a record of Israel's sacred history, called *Jewish Antiquities*. Originally a devout Jew, and a leader in the revolt against Rome, he became a strong supporter of the Flavian dynasty of Roman rule and read both the war and the history of Israel from that perspective. The best edition of his work is H. St. J. Thackeray, Ralph Marcus, and Louis H. Feldman, eds., *Josephus*, 9 vols., Loeb Classical Library (London/Cambridge, MA: William Heinemann/Harvard University Press, 1926-1965). The passage on Herod and John the Baptist is found in volume 9, pages 81-85.

20 See John P. Meier, *A Marginal Jew. Rethinking the Historical Jesus*, 5 vols., Anchor Yale Bible Reference Library (New York/New Haven: Doubleday/Yale University Press, 1991-2016), 2:171-76. Meier rightly argues against any attempt to harmonize Mark and Josephus, insisting that, "Josephus is to be preferred for history; Mark is to be mined for tradition history and theological intent" (p. 175).

his life, but announces the present and future coming of God as King (see 14:58, 60-62). Yet there is a difference between John and Jesus. After the slaying and the ghoulish presentation of the head upon a dish (vv. 27-28), Mark's account of John the Baptist's death closes as his body is taken by his disciples and laid in a tomb (v. 29). According to vv. 14-16, rumors of the resurrection of the Baptist are in the air; but they are only rumors. The Christian community reading this story believes that Jesus has been slain, buried, and has been raised from the dead (see 16:1-8). There is no such Christian tradition surrounding the figure of John the Baptist.

Once this is clear, then the theological and literary function of vv. 14-29 within the context of vv. 6b-30 emerges. Mark uses his traditions concerning the death of John the Baptist for at least two reasons. John the Baptist is the messenger of God (see 1:2-3), the one who announces Jesus (vv. 7-8). He has an unswerving commitment to his God-given mission: to preach a baptism of repentance for the forgiveness of sins (1:4). This mission has cost him his life (6:17-29). Secondly, his life and death have close parallels with the life and death of Jesus.

The disciples have appeared regularly to this point in the story (see 1:16-20; 2:13-14; 3:13-19, 20-35; 4:10-11, 33-34). They have already had a moment of weak faith on the stormy sea (4:35-41) to which we shall briefly return. The audience is aware that *unconditional commitment to God's design and being a follower of Jesus* should mark the life of the Twelve, at present out on their mission (vv. 7-13). It is also made clear for the first time, by means of this interlude, that discipleship will cost no less than everything (see 8:31–9:1). As followers of Jesus, they are called to share in the destiny of Jesus (see 8:34-35), prophetically acted out in the martyrdom of John the Baptist. "John's martyrdom not only prefigured Jesus' death, it also prefigures the death of anyone who would come after him!"[21] We turn to v. 30 with this message ringing in the ears of listener and in the minds and hearts of the audience.

Mark 6:30

Those who were sent out in v. 7 return and gather around Jesus in v. 30. The returning Twelve adopt a physical position around Jesus which is reminiscent of the "being with him" of 3:14. But the rest of the passage indicates that they have not understood what has happened to them, and what they have done. Using a strong verb (*apēngeilan*), they "announce" their achievements to Jesus (see also 5:14, 19; 16:10, 13). They regard themselves as the masters of the situation, informing Jesus of "all that they had done, and all that they had taught" (v. 30b. AT). The Twelve transfer the authority for their success *to themselves*. Despite the focus upon Jesus as the one who authorizes and sends in vv. 7-13, they report in v. 30 "everything" that *they* did and everything that *they* said. This is to miss the point of their being *sent by Jesus* on a mission (3:14b-15; 6:7-13) which will only be an effective proclamation of the kingdom (however "successful" it might appear) if they are "with Jesus" (3:14a).

There is deep irony in the fact that the returning missionaries report to the one who authorized them (see 3:15; 6:7), telling him all the things "they" have done and said. The audience knows that their missionary activity depends entirely upon the one to whom they are announcing their success. The essential qualities of a true disciple have been made clear by means of the episode of the death of the Baptist (vv. 14-29: the middle of the sandwich). Not only are they authorized by Jesus, but like the Baptist, they must accept the destiny the following of Jesus necessarily brings. There is nothing of this in

---

[21] Edwards, "Markan Sandwiches," 206.

the report of the Twelve as they come back from their mission. They are unable to recognize that they have associated themselves with Jesus in a mission that has to do with the reigning presence *of God* (v. 6b), cost what it may (vv. 14-29). They come back flushed with their success. They have failed as disciples of Jesus.

True to their call which comes to them from God through Jesus (1:16-20; 3:13-19), and like the Baptist, the disciples are to commit themselves unflinchingly to the mission for which they have been empowered by their association with Jesus (6:7-13). As with the Baptist, it will cost them no less than everything (vv. 14-29). They fail. They return to Jesus, the source of all that they do and say, with whose mission they are privileged to be associated (6:6b-7), to tell him everything *they* have said and done (v. 30).

A short time before this episode, as Jesus stilled the stormy seas, he questioned the faith of his disciples: "Why are you afraid? Have you no faith?" (4:40). This was the first indication of the limitations of the fragile human beings called to be disciples of Jesus. Up to this point they have responded immediately to his call (1:16-20; 2:13-14; 3:13-19), and accompanied him on his wandering mission as healer, preacher and wonder worker (1:17–4:34). But after the calming of the storm, filled with awe and puzzlement, they ask one another, "Who is this then, that even the wind and sea obey him?" (4:41).

They are not able to understand *who Jesus is*. More miracles follow (5:1-43), and Jesus' own townsfolk ask the right question: "Where did this man get all this?" (6:2), but they are not able to go beyond his local trade, his mother and his siblings (v. 3). But what of the Twelve, instituted by Jesus (3:14-19), what of the "new family" of Jesus (see 3:34-35)? Mark 6:6b-30 takes the dramatic presentation of the disciples and the Twelve one step further. Now the Twelve, chosen from among the disciples (see 3:13), are not able to understand *who they are*! This passage plays a strategic role in the instruction of the members of Mark's missionary audience. They have followed the disciples' initial successes (see 1:16-20; 2:13-14; 3:13-19; 6:6b-13), through their doubt (see 4:41), via the account of the death of the Baptist (6:14-19), into failure (6:30). But the surprising end of Mark's story (16:1-8) will lead the audience beyond their failures.

MARK 16:1-8

Mark's resurrection story is the briefest and most surprising resurrection account in the New Testament. In common with the other Gospels, he reports the visit of the women on the first day of the week (Sunday) (16:1-2), the discovery of an empty tomb (vv. 3-4), and the communication of the Easter message that the crucified Jesus has been raised by God. He is no longer in a place of death (vv. 5-6). Recalling a promise made at the final meal (14:28), they are commissioned to tell the disciples and Peter that Jesus is going before them into Galilee. There they will see him (v. 7). *But they are so terrified that they flee from the tomb and tell no one* (v. 8). The Gospel of Mark ends with a message of women who have stood by Jesus from his Galilean mission to his death and resurrection, unlike the male disciples who all fled in fear at Jesus' arrest (14:50). But, in the end, even they also fail![22]

Mark's Christian audience, aware of the traditions about the report of the women to the disciples (see Matt 28:8; Luke 24:9; John 20:2. See also 1 Cor 15:3-8), know that Mark has changed the ending of the traditional story. Although it may appear odd to us, Mark does this to remain consistent with his overall message of disciples and missionaries.

---

[22] Commentators have often suggested that the Gospel could not end that way and claim that the original ending had been lost. Against this suggestion, see Francis J. Moloney, *The Gospel of Mark. A Commentary* (Grand Rapids: Baker Academic, 2012), 340-41.

They cannot succeed on the basis of their own wisdom and authority. As Jesus shared his final meal with his disciples he told them: "You will all become deserters; for it is written, 'I will strike the shepherd and the sheep will be scattered.' But after I am raised up I will go before you into Galilee" (14:28). *The Word of Jesus* promises that he will go before them into Galilee. This word is recalled by the young man at the tomb: "He is going ahead of you into Galilee; there you will see him, just as he told you" (16:7). The future tense of 14:28 ("I will go before you into Galilee") has become a present tense in 16:7 ("He is going before you into Galilee"). The disciples and the women may fail as they flee in fear (14:50; 16:8), but *the Word of Jesus never fails*.

MISSION

The fact that we have the Gospel of Mark indicates that – beyond and after the story as it is told – the disciples, Peter, and the women will see Jesus in Galilee. It *must* happen, as Jesus has said that it *would* happen. But such an encounter does not take place because the disciples or the women are successful in their mission. It will happen because of the power of God and the never-failing promise of the Word of Jesus. Mark's Gospel closes with a *promise* that an encounter with the risen Lord lies ahead of them. It will take place whenever and however God decides. It does not depend upon us. The promise of Jesus will not be thwarted. The life-giving encounter with the risen Jesus can only be found somewhere in Galilee, in a future meeting between the risen Lord and the fragile disciples, men and women (see 14:28; 16:7). There they will see him, as he promised, despite the failure of everyone in the story, including the women who had accompanied him from Jerusalem, through the Cross and into an empty tomb (15:47; 16:1-4). No matter how dramatic even their failure at the tomb might appear to be (see 16:8), they (we) will see him (see 14:28; 16:7). But that, of course, is a story to which we all belong. Mark 1:1–16:8 tells of Jesus' calling (1:16-20), commissioning (3:13-19), and sending out of missionaries (6:6b-30). The ministry of the missionary is to repeat the ministry of Jesus. It will cost no less than everything, as the execution of John the Baptist instructs us (6:13-29).

Mark's story ends with a message of human failure and divine success. Contrary to the understanding of the Twelve who have been commissioned in 3:13-19, and then sent out on mission in 6:6b-30, it is not the skill and the authority of the missionary that makes an apostle (see v. 30), but the loving and powerful presence of our God who goes before us into our Galilees (14:28; 16:7). There we will see him, as he promises. It is as frail servants of a loving God who always goes before us that we can best serve those to whom we have been sent. Henri Nouwen caught this truth in the title and the message of his valuable book on contemporary ministry: *The Wounded Healer*.[23] In our failure we can repeat the words of St. Paul: "But he said to me, 'My grace is sufficient for you, for power is made perfect in weakness.' So I will boast all the more gladly of my weaknesses, so that the power of Christ may dwell in me. Therefore, I am content with weaknesses, insults, hardships, persecutions, and calamities for the sake of Christ; for whenever I am weak, then I am strong" (2 Cor 12:9-10).[24] Without Christ we can do nothing (see John 15:5). With him, we can do anything; for everything is possible with God (see Mark 10:27; Luke 1:37).[25]

---

[23] Henri Nouwen, *The Wounded Healer. Ministry in Contemporary Society* (New York: Doubleday Image Books, 1979).

[24] It is often suggested that these two earliest Christian witnesses (Paul [50-64 CE] and Mark [70 CE]) share this fundamental view of the unconditional primacy of God's gracious initiative in the Christian life. See, for example, Joel Marcus, "Mark - Interpreter of Paul," *New Testament Studies* 46 (2000): 473-87.

[25] For further reflection upon this statement, see my essay "'He Is Going before You into Galilee.' Mark 16:6-8 and the Christian Community," in *Gospel Interpretation and Christian Life*, Scholars Collection 3 (Adelaide: ATF Theology, 2017), 117-30.

3

THE GOSPEL OF MATTHEW

The Turning Point of the Ages: "Make disciples of all nations" (Matt 28:19)

Most New Testament specialists suggest that when Matthew was writing his Gospel, he used Mark, and perhaps a now lost document that we call "Q."[1] Matthew follows Mark more closely than Luke, and there is much in the Christology and theology of Matthew that he received from Mark. However, his so-called "ecclesiology" is unique. His understanding of the community of believers, which only he calls "Church" (see 16:18; 18:17; Greek: *ecclesia*), favored a New Testament model understanding of the Church in those communities that have bishops. This is especially true for the Roman Catholic Church that is strongly determined by its Petrine leadership, its sense of hierarchy and teaching authority (see Matt 16:13-19; 18:18-20). Another unique feature, side-by-side with his early understanding of a teaching

---

[1] On this "two source theory," with Mark as the first Gospel to be written (about 70 CE) and Matthew and Luke following his basic story (in the late 80s CE), with help from a now lost further document that we call "Q," the first letter of the German word "Quelle," meaning "source," see Brown and Moloney, *Interpreting the New Testament*, 113-24.

Church is the absence of a mission to the Gentiles during Jesus' public ministry, and the limitation of the mission of the disciples to "the lost sheep of the house of Israel" (10:6).[2]

GO NOWHERE AMONG THE GENTILES

Matthew repeats Mark's account of the calling of the first disciples in Mark 1:16-20 and 2:17 (see Matt 4:18-22; 9:9 [where Mark's name "Levi" is changed to "Matthew"]), and he commissions the Twelve (10:1). However, Matthew omits their being sent out on mission during his ministry (see Mark 6:6b-30). In the second major narrative unit of his Gospel, dedicated to Jesus' ministry of preaching, teaching and healing (Matt 4:17–11:1), "the disciples" accompany Jesus as he begins his Galilean ministry (Matt 5:1-2).[3] But at this stage of his story of Jesus Matthew avoids Mark's presentation of the disciples actively involved in missionary activity. A long discourse on mission closes the narrative unit (10:1–11:1), during which Jesus instructs the disciples in the story (and the audience) on the challenges of a future mission, and the way Christian disciples must face such challenges. But there is no description of any missionary activity; the passage is made up entirely of Jesus' instructions, as the disciples (and the audience) listen. Startlingly, at the beginning of that discourse on the mission of the Church (10:1–11:1), he instructs his disciples: "Go nowhere among the Gentiles, and into no town of the Samaritans, but go rather to the lost sheep of the house of Israel" (10:5-6).

---

2   For an earlier presentation of the following, without focus on the theme of mission, see Francis J. Moloney, *The Resurrection of the Messiah. A Narrative Commentary on the Resurrection Narratives in the Four Gospels* (New York: Paulist, 2015), 33-68.

3   For a description of Matthew's careful literary technique in telling his story of Jesus through six "narrative units" (1 = 1:1–4:16; 2 = 4:17–11:1; 3 = 11:2–16:12; 4 = 16:13–20:34; 5 = 21:1–28:15; 6 = 28:16–20), see Francis J. Moloney, *The Living Voice of the Gospel. The Gospels Today*, 2nd ed. (Mulgrave, VIC: John Garratt, 2006), 107-19.

Mark dedicates a long section of his story to Jesus' activities among the Gentiles. He cures the daughter of a Syrophoenician woman in "the region of Tyre" (7:24-30), journeys by way of the pagan cities of Tyre and Sidon, through the Gentile Decapolis (Greek cities on the north-eastern side of the Lake of Galilee) and cures a deaf mute there (7:31-37). On the Gentile side of the lake, he feeds a multitude of Gentiles because "some of them have come from a great distance" (8:1-9).[4] For Matthew, Jesus never moves outside the geographical confines of the land of Israel. In the narrative unit that describes the intensification of the crisis of Jesus' ministry (11:2–16:12), Mark's Syrophoenician woman (Mark 7:26) is described as a Canaanite woman (Matt 15:22).[5] She comes to Jesus from the region of Tyre and Sidon, asking that he heal her daughter. His first response, describing his own ministry, matches the command that he gave to his disciples at the beginning of his missionary discourse: "I was sent only to the lost sheep of the house of Israel" (15:24. See 10:5-6).[6]

This limited missionary outreach only to the lost sheep of Israel, however, appears to be compromised by two miracles that Jesus works for Gentiles during his ministry. Matthew reports the healing of the Gentile centurion's servant (8:5-13), during his Galilean ministry of teaching and healing. However, even though Jesus responds positively to the centurion and subsequently cures the servant of a Gentile soldier, this action runs against the grain of the rest of his mission "only to the lost sheep of Israel." The miracle is worked within the

---

[4] For a detailed presentation of this section of Mark's story as dedicated to the Gentile mission of Jesus, see Moloney, *The Gospel of Mark*, 144-57.

[5] Historically, the description "Canaanite" is the same as "Syrophoenician," but most likely reflects a better awareness on the part of Matthew of the local name for people from that region. See Ulrich Luz, *Matthew*, trans. James E. Crouch, 3 vols., Hermeneia (Minneapolis: Fortress, 2001-2007), 2:338-39.

[6] This limitation of Jesus' ministry to "the lost sheep of Israel" does not appear in Mark's Gospel.

context of lack of belief in Israel (see 8:1-27). It may be the curing of a Gentile, but it is used by Matthew as a warning against Israel:

> Truly, I say to you, not even in Israel have I found such faith. I tell you many will come from east and west and sit at the table of Abraham, Isaac and Jacob while the sons of the kingdom will be thrown into the outer darkness; there men will weep and gnash their teeth. (vv. 10-12)

Despite Jesus' personal mission to Israel alone (15:24), his words address a future situation when both Jesus and his disciples will be rejected by God's chosen people. A time will come, Jesus indicates by this miracle, when they will be rejected by "the sons of the kingdom," and sent on a mission to peoples "from east and west" (see 28:16-20).[7] Strangely, it will be those to whom the kingdom had been given who will be cast into darkness, while many "from east and west" will be seated at the table of Abraham. But at this stage of the story, the healing of a centurion's servant is a promise of things to come.

A similar point is made later in the story, as anger against Jesus increases. As we have already seen, in Matthew 15:21-28, the audience finds an encounter between Jesus and a Gentile, the Canaanite woman. He cures her daughter. At the end of Jesus' encounter with the Gentile woman Jesus explains why she has been granted her request: "O woman, great is your faith! Be it done for you as you desire" (v. 28). Jesus directs these words to the Canaanite woman herself because of her humble and accepting faith. Before the miracle is worked she has identified herself as deserving nothing, but nevertheless requests: "dogs

---

[7] The aggressive nature of Jesus' response to the Gentile centurion's request, a warning against the faithlessness of Israel, is especially obvious when one compares Luke's longer development of the same miracle tradition (Luke 7:1-10 [thus from "Q"]) in a setting of miracles and instructions that confirm his identity through saving acts. See John T. Carroll, *Luke. A Commentary*, The New Testament Library (Louisville: Westminster John Knox, 2012), 158-63.

eating the crumbs that fall from the master's table." Jesus' meeting with the Canaanite woman is located between two miraculous feeding miracles (see 14:15-21; 15:32-38). The woman asks to be allowed to share, however minimally, in the gracious gift of Jesus' unique mission to Israel (see 15:23-27).[8] A Gentile is used to instruct the true Israel, for Matthew the Christian community, on authentic faith.

Despite the miracles worked for two Gentiles, the Gentile centurion and the Canaanite woman, disciples are to go nowhere among the Gentiles (10:5-6), and the mission of Jesus and his disciples is limited to the lost sheep of Israel (15:24). But a threat hangs over the lost sheep (8:12). Although the Gospel of Matthew was probably written in Antioch to address a largely Jewish-Christian audience late in the 80s of the first century, many who received it would have been aware of the gradual increase of Gentiles who were being drawn into the Christian circle.[9]

Looking back upon the life of Jesus, they regard him as someone who never swerved in his passionate perfection of the Law and the Prophets (see 5:17-18). Now faced with the presence of Gentiles in the community, they also recall a tradition of a commission that the risen Jesus gave to the eleven disciples on a mountain in Galilee. There he commissioned them to preach the Gospel to all nations (28:16-20). How had the tension between the limited missionary activity of Jesus and his disciples during his ministry been transformed into his sending of his disciples on a universal mission (28:16-20)? Why has Matthew developed his theology of mission in this way?

---

[8] For a more detailed study of the two bread miracles in Matthew, and their literary and theological context, see Moloney, *A Body Broken for a Broken People*, 107-15.
[9] See Moloney, *The Living Voice*, 119-23.

UNTIL HEAVEN AND EARTH PASS AWAY

As the public ministry of Jesus opened, he embraced the best traditions of first-century Judaism, forging a close bond between his followers and the observance of the Law. Early in his Sermon on the Mountain, he announced:

> Think not that I have come to abolish the Law and the Prophets; I have not come to abolish them, but to fulfill them. For truly, I say to you, till heaven and earth pass away, not an iota, not a dot will pass from the Law until all is accomplished. (5:17-18)

A crucial *temporal* element is introduced into the narrative. An important feature of any narrative is the way an author uses various aspects of "time" as the plot of the story unfolds.[10] Generally, the events in a narrative are reported in the chronological order in which they happen in a human story. Events follow one another down an acceptable and understandable timeline. This use of time is generally called "narrative time." Reading through (or listening to) narrative time, the audience moves from one event to another, from one day to another, one year to another, until the end of the story is reached. In an ideal biography, the reader moves satisfyingly and systematically from the subject's parents and background, birth, life story, death, and subsequent evaluation.

But sometimes events from the past are recalled, drawn into the story to enrich the events of "narrative time" as they unfold. Two well-known examples of this are found in the story in the Gospel of John that tells of John the Baptist's experience at Jesus' baptism (John 1:32-34) and the fact that a man was born blind (9:1-5). They are reported,

---

10 For more detailed presentation of the narrative theory that follows, Rimmon-Kenan, *Narrative Fiction*, 43-58.

even though they are past events. The chronologically determined reporting of events (narrative time) is enriched by recalling events that took place *outside* that chronology, and *prior to it*. This practice of looking back into a time *prior* to the "narrative time" of the regular passing of events in a story is called "analepsis."

More important for the interpretation of Matthew, however, is a tension we have sensed in the limitation of the ministry of the disciples and Jesus, closing with a mission to the whole world. For the audience, this tension is heightened by a hint of something that will happen in the future. In all the Gospels, Jesus' predictions of his oncoming passion and resurrection (Mark 8:31, 9:31, 10:32-34; parrs.; John 3:14; 8:28; 12:32) are excellent examples of this technique. Information concerning Jesus' suffering and vindication creates a sense of expectancy in a reader who follows the narrative, waiting for the accomplishment of these promised events. The technical term used for these interruptions into "narrative time" that point to some *future* event is "prolepsis."

In the technical language used by literary critics, the natural and logical time sequence of a story is called "narrative time." The insertions into the narrative that look back to an earlier period ("analepses") or forward to a time beyond the limitations of what the audience has been told at that point ("prolepses") are called "plotted time."

Jesus' programmatic words to his disciples in 5:17-18 come very early in Jesus' story. They open his Sermon on the Mount, and they contain a powerful prolepsis: words that look beyond the timeline of the narrative, into the plotted time of the future.

> Think not that I have come to abolish the law and the prophets; I have come not to abolish them but to fulfill them. For truly, I say to you, *till heaven and earth pass away*, not an iota, not a dot, will pass from the law *until all is accomplished*.

The two expressions of time ("till" ... "until") in the passage refer to some future "time." In the original Greek the same word is used twice to point to the future: *heōs an*. Although they are translated into English as "till" and "until," both uses of the same Greek expression look forward to some "time" in the future. Jesus' preaching during his public ministry is being faithfully reported (narrative time), but his words introduce a time "yet to come" when the present order of things will be changed: heaven and earth will pass away and all will be accomplished. These expressions refer to a time in the future *until* which every detail of the Mosaic Law must be observed: "*till* heaven and earth pass away ... *until* all is accomplished."[11] When might that future time be? In the light of our Christian understanding of the end of time, essential to Pauline teaching (see 1 Thess 1:9b-10; 4:13-18) and Jesus' teaching in the Gospels, beginning in Mark 13 and strongly reaffirmed in Matthew 24–25, many interpreters read 5:17-18 as a reference to the traditional Jewish notion of the end of time. They suggest that, for the Matthean Christians, the Law must be observed in its entirety till the end of time.[12]

This understanding of the future events referred to in 5:17-18 can look to Jesus' limitation of his disciples' and his own preaching to the lost sheep of Israel (10:5-6; 15:24), and his hesitation before working two miracles for Gentiles (8:5-13; 15:21-28) for support. For these interpreters, all Christians are to observe every detail of the Jewish Law till the end of time.[13] However, Matthew's resurrection story brings some awkward contradictions. Jesus' final words in the

---

[11] See John P. Meier, *Law and History in Matthew's Gospel*, Analecta Biblica 71 (Rome: Biblical Institute Press, 1976), 48: "It is important for the subsequent exegesis that 'until' is the *only* possible meaning. There are no solid grounds for changing the meaning to 'in order that'."

[12] See, for example, the authoritative interpretations of William D. Davies and Dale C. Allison, *The Gospel According to Saint Matthew*, 3 vols., International Critical Commentary (Edinburgh: T. & T. Clark, 1988-1997), 1:482-503, and Luz, *Matthew*, 1:213-19.

[13] The strongest contemporary advocate of this position is David Sim, *The Gospel of Matthew and Christian Judaism. The History and Social Setting of the Matthean Community*, Studies in the New Testament and Its World (Edinburgh: T. & T. Clark, 1998).

Gospel of Matthew send the disciples on a mission to the ends of the earth and promise that he will be with them till the close of the age (28:16-20). If the future time of 5:17-18 referred to the end of all time, the command of Jesus that the Jewish Law be perfectly observed, without changing even the tiniest detail, would still be in force in the post-Easter Matthean Community, awaiting Jesus' final coming. But if the risen Jesus sends the disciples out on mission to the Gentiles (28:16-20), what has happened in the meantime? Obviously: the death and resurrection of Jesus.[14]

MATTHEW'S PASSION STORY

As is the case with much of the Gospel of Matthew, his passion narrative depends very heavily on his main source, the Gospel of Mark. Matthew *accepts* the Markan account, and all that it suggests but into this basic structure and message Matthew has inserted some unique features. We can focus upon only three of them: his description of the death of Jesus (27:45-54), the resurrection of Jesus (28:1-4), and the final commission of the risen Jesus (28:16-20).

Matthew 27:45-54

In 27:45-54 Matthew reports the death of Jesus with additions that appear nowhere else in the New Testament. As Jesus dies (vv. 45-50), Matthew claims that his death is accompanied by "apocalyptic" signs, symbolic end-time events that mark the passing away of heaven and earth:

> From noon on, darkness came over the whole land until three in the afternoon ... Then Jesus cried again with a loud voice and breathed his last. And behold the curtain

---

[14] The interpretation that follows depends upon the work of Meier, *Law and History*, 1-40. See also John P. Meier, *The Vision of Matthew. Christ, Church and Morality in the First Gospel*, Theological Inquiries (New York: Paulist, 1978), 26-39.

of the temple was torn in two, from top to bottom. The earth shook and the rocks were split. The tombs also were opened and many bodies of the saints who had fallen asleep were raised. After his resurrection they came out of the tombs, and entered the holy city and appeared to many. (vv. 45, 50-53)

Unlike Mark 15:39, where only the centurion sees the events that accompany the death of Jesus, in Matthew, all those keeping watch with him (Matt 25:35-36: Roman soldiers) "saw the earthquake and what took place, they were filled with awe, and said, 'Truly, this was the Son of God'" (v. 54). The collection of end-time phenomena that accompany Jesus' death and lead to the confession of the centurion and his companions are found only in Matthew: the splitting of the rocks, the opening of the tombs, the resurrection of the deceased holy ones, and their appearance in the Holy City after the resurrection of Jesus.

This is the beginning of the promise made by Jesus in 5:17-18: the Law must be observed in all its detail *until heaven and earth pass away*. Some of Mark's imagery is repeated: the darkness over the earth and the tearing of the veil, but Matthew has added to this scenario considerably. He has drawn upon "end-time" symbols from Jewish tradition, but he has *shifted their timing*.[15] The events described – darkening of the skies, splitting of the rocks, and the rising of the dead – are events that were expected at the end of all time when God would return as Lord and Judge (see Amos 8:9; Joel 2:10; Hag 2:6; Zech 14:5; Dan 12:2; Jer 15:9; Ezek 37:7, 12-13; Isa 26:19; Dan 12:2). Matthew indicates that these events will take place *not only* at the

---

15 The expression "apocalyptic" is used to describe events that are traditionally associated with the final and definitive intervention of God *at the end of time*. As it is about the action of God, highly symbolic language is found. See John P. Meier, *Matthew*, New Testament Message 3 (Wilmington, DE: Michael Glazier, 1980), 350-53; Donald Senior, *The Passion of Jesus in the Gospel of Matthew*, The Passion Series 1 (Wilmington, DE: Michael Glazier, 1985), 142-49.

end of all history, as was held by Jewish tradition. They have *already happened* at the death of Jesus. Heaven and earth are passing away! But this is only the beginning. A forward-looking tension emerges as the passion narrative draws to a close. The reader is told that the holy ones who rise from their open graves go into the city "after his resurrection." The story has not come to closure as the audience has been advised – already at Jesus' death – that he will rise (v. 53).

Matthew 28:1-4

Matthew's resurrection story leapfrogs between reports of negative responses to the resurrection (the setting of the guard at the tomb in 27:62-66, and the development of the lie that disciples stole the body in 28:11-15) interspersed with the proclamation of Easter (the event of the resurrection and Jesus' appearance to the women in 28:1-10, and the commissioning of the disciples on the mountain in Galilee in 28:16-20). In 28:1-4 Matthew provides the only attempt in the New Testament to offer a description of events that surrounded the resurrection of Jesus. All others, Paul, Mark, Luke and John, report that he was crucified, buried, an empty tomb was discovered, and (with the exception of Mark) that he appeared to his disciples as their risen Lord. They do not attempt to describe events that accompanied the resurrection of Jesus.

Matthew 28:1 opens the resurrection story by focusing on the fact that what follows takes place "after the Sabbath ... on the first day of the week," thus three days after the death of Jesus. The women making the journey to the tomb, "Mary Magdalene and the other Mary" are those who saw where he was buried (27:61: "Mary and the other Mary"). He refers to the time of the day and the rising of the sun in v. 1. "The literal dawning of a new day signals a new period of history."[16]

---

16 Davies and Allison, *Matthew*, 3:664.

Having set the scene in this very precise fashion, Matthew describes events that accompanied the resurrection of Jesus in a way reminiscent of the end-time language used at Jesus' death in 27:51-54.

> And behold, there was a great earthquake; for an angel of the Lord descended from heaven and came and rolled back the stone and sat upon it. His appearance was like lightning, and his raiment white as snow. And for fear of him the guards trembled and became like dead men. (28:2-4)

As the death of Jesus was marked by a scenario associated with the end of the ages, the same apocalyptic language returns at Jesus' resurrection. Yet another earthquake takes place (see Hag 2:6; Zech 14:5), an angel of the Lord with an appearance like lightning descends from heaven (see 1 Enoch 1:3-9; 20:17-19), and trembling and fear possesses the guards (see Dan 10:7-9, 16; 12:2). "Matthew extends into the empty tomb story the apocalyptic atmosphere that erupted at the moment of Jesus' death."[17] There can be no mistaking Matthew's intentions. By associating events that traditionally were predicted to mark the end of all time, Matthew points to the death and resurrection of Jesus, not as the end of all time, but as the turning point of the ages.[18] Everything that has been in place until this *time* is being transformed, because heaven and earth are passing away (see 5:18a). Everything has been accomplished (see 5:18b). "The essential link between the death-resurrection of Jesus and the beginning of the new age strains Matthew's narration. He wants to show that God's acts of salvation come immediately as a response to the obedient death of Jesus."[19]

---

[17] Donald Senior, *Matthew*, Abingdon New Testament Commentaries (Nashville, TN: Abingdon, 1998), 340. See also, Meier, *Matthew*, 359-63.

[18] See Eduard Schweizer, *The Good News According to Matthew*, trans. David E. Green (London: SPCK, 1976), 524: "All the elements (of vv. 2-4) thus recall the signs expected to accompany the coming of the Lord at the end of the world and the irruption of the Kingdom of God."

[19] Senior, *The Passion of Jesus in the Gospel of Matthew*, 147.

Matthew does not claim that the world as we know it has come to an end. His Gospel begins with Jesus' programmatic description of a Christian lifestyle in the Sermon on the Mount (5:1–7:28), and he warns that there is still much to be done, and much to be endured (see 24:9-14, 36-51). Matthew's audience knows that it is in for the long haul. However, by marking Jesus' death (27:51-54) and resurrection (28:2-4) with events that were traditionally associated with the end-time, he insists on what we might call an "anticipated end-time." No longer will God enter definitively into human history *only* at the end of all time; he has anticipated that entry in Jesus' death and resurrection. After all, as the audience learned from the infancy story, Jesus of Nazareth is the Emmanuel, God with us (1:23), a theme that will return as the Gospel ends: "I am with you always, to the end of the age" (28:20).

The passing of time and the events of humankind will continue as history unfolds, but everything has been transformed by Jesus' death and resurrection. This suggests to the audience that Jesus' earlier instructions that all details of the Law must be observed (5:17-20), and that *the time* of his disciples' limitation of their mission to Israel (see 10:5-6) has come to an end. He had come only to the lost sheep of Israel, and there he has lived out the righteousness of God in its fullness (see 15:2-4). Another *time* is at hand because of the crucifixion and resurrection of Jesus. At the very beginning of the story, John the Baptist objected to Jesus' submission to his baptism. But Jesus replied: "Let it be so for now; for thus it is fitting for us to fulfill all righteousness" (3:15). That "for now" has come to an end at the death and resurrection of Jesus, for Matthew and his community, the turning point of the ages. One era has come to an end; another is dawning.

Matthew 28:16-20

The final scene in the Gospel of Matthew, the commissioning of the disciples for mission, and Jesus' promise to be with them, is a key to the interpretation of the Gospel itself. "All of the basic theological statements of the Gospel of Matthew seem to be gathered up in these forty words at the end of the Gospel."[20] We have seen that Jesus' ministry was directed uniquely to Israel (15:25), and that he also limited his disciples' ministry to the lost sheep of the house of Israel (10:5-6). Even the two episodes where he worked miracles at the request of Gentiles (8:5-13: curing of the centurion's servant; 15:21-28: curing of the child of the Canaanite woman) are used by Matthew to criticize Israel's lack of faith.

Indeed, as he opened his Sermon on the Mount, he taught that every detail of the Law and the Prophets must be taught and observed (5:17-20). However, in the final commission, this limited mission program, and the agenda of the Law and the Prophets, seem to have been transcended. The key to understanding 28:16-20 lies in the interpretation of the death and resurrection of Jesus as the turning point of the ages, as only now have heaven and earth passed away, and all is accomplished (see 5:18). With the dramatic (and apocalyptic) events of his death (27:51-54) and resurrection (28:2-4) behind him, Jesus can go to the mountain in Galilee to meet his eleven disciples.

The "prolepsis," that tension in the temporal aspect of narrative that must look further into the story for its "time," has been resolved. Matthew 28:16-20 does more than resolve the prolepsis initiated in 5:17-20. It takes the reader into a new time that lies outside the time-limitations of the story of the Gospel, a time that could be called,

---

20 Luz, *Matthew*, 3:621.

in pseudo-Matthean language, "the time of the Church" (see Matt 16:18; 18:17).[21]

It is impossible fully to appreciate the vigor of 28:16-20 without understanding the setting within which this Gospel was proclaimed. The Matthean community was caught in a difficult situation of rejection from their traditional Jewish world and its familiar ways. Matthew's response to this pastoral situation was to present Jesus as the one who continues and fulfills God's design. The people in the synagogue, who reject Matthew's Christians, continue the tradition of the Jewish leaders and the people in the story of Jesus who rejected him. They not only rejected him, but they crucified him, crying out for his death to a vacillating Pilate, who preferred to wash his hands of the whole business (Matt 27:15-26).

The Matthean Christians of the late first century were struggling to identify themselves over against their former neighbors and kinsfolk, who had rejected them. Their predecessors had crucified Jesus. The Christians, most of whom were Jews, had to face a future without the support and comfort of their traditional faith and practice. However, Jewish religion at this period was also searching for its post-war and post-Jerusalem Temple religious identity. Gradually they were generating a firm adherence to the Law that would eventually produce what later came to be known as Rabbinic Judaism, but it was embryonic toward the end of the first century. It is most powerfully articulated in the *Mishnah* (third century), and the great Jerusalem and Babylonian *Talmudim* (fourth and fifth centuries, respectively). But the Jewish community at the time of Matthew's Gospel was only an embryonic form of what later became one of the world's great religions, based upon the magnificent systems, theology, liturgical life

---

21 Senior, *Matthew*, 344, comments: "The resurrection marks the beginning of the final age of the world."

and spirituality that developed from such documents as the *Mishnah* and the *Talmudim*.[22]

The Gospel of Matthew emerges in a time when two religions, once identified as one religion, were searching for their identity. On the one hand, the Matthean Christians are being told a story that affirms that Jesus is the perfection of all righteousness, the one who generates the true Israel. This tradition eventually became Christianity, and the Gospel of Matthew part of its "Sacred Scripture." On the other hand, an emerging post-war Judaism attaches itself closer to the observance of Torah and its ordinances, finding there a path of truth and life. This tradition eventually became Judaism, based upon Torah and its interpretation in the other books of the Bible and later Jewish rabbinic commentary.[23] In this setting, as paths separated, hostility and rejection were part of a tense relationship between Jews and Christians.

Evidence for this late first-century tension between Matthean Christians and the local Jewish community can be sensed throughout the Gospel of Matthew. They lie behind the very negative presentation, often by Jesus himself, of the Pharisees and the Scribes (see 23:1-26). These difficulties generated the terrible and angry words uttered by the leaders of Israel during Jesus' trial: "His blood be on us and on our children" (27:25). Such words reflect the tense atmosphere and the hostility between Christian and Jew late in the 80s of the first century, not from the time of Jesus.[24]

---

[22] Excellent English translations of these important Jewish texts can be found in Herbert Danby, *The Mishnah. Translated from the Hebrew with Brief Explanatory Notes* (Oxford: Oxford University Press, 1938), and Isidore Epstein, trans. and ed., *The Babylonian Talmud*, 35 vols. (London: Soncino, 1948-1952).

[23] On this, see the important work of Martin Goodman, *A History of Judaism* (London: Allen Lane, 2017), 229-88. Goodman concludes: "The legacy of the religious system crafted by the rabbinic schools over the thousand years after 70 CE has been fundamental to most later forms of Judaism" (p. 288).

[24] For a more detailed explanation of this terrible passage, see Moloney, *The Resurrection of the Messiah*, 39-41.

What we find in Matthew 28:16-20, however, is not hostile; it transcends all such concerns as the Matthean community moves further away from Judaism into a Gentile mission. These words direct the Matthean disciples, and those reading and hearing the words of the risen Jesus, into a way of life that looked beyond major religious thought and practice of late first-century Jews. With this historical and religious background in mind, Matthew's final episode speaks eloquently to the new Israel, sent out on mission to all the nations (28:16-20).

Eleven disciples (as Judas has left the Twelve in despair [27:3-10]) went into Galilee, to the mountain, already instructed by Jesus to meet him there (v. 16). This is not the first time Jesus has summoned his disciples to the top of a mountain to give them important instructions. Earlier in the Gospel (5:1–7:28) he began his ministry of teaching by gathering his disciples on a mountain (see 5:1) to give them a new Law (see 5:17-20, 21-22, 27-28, 31-32, 33-34, 38-39, 43-44). On a new Sinai a new and perfect Moses gave a new people of God a new Law. The situating of the giving of the new Law on a mountain was important for Matthew (see 4:8-9; 5:1-2; 7:28-29; 17:6-7). On mountains, closer to God, the human can touch the divine. As Jesus began his Sermon on the Mount he insisted that, for the moment, the Law and the Prophets had to be lived perfectly (5:17-20). But he indicates that there will be a time when heaven and earth pass away, when all is accomplished. At that time, all such limitations to traditional Jewish life and practice could no longer hold universal sway. As we have seen, for Matthew heaven and earth are rocked and the signs of the end of all time are present at Jesus' death (27:45, 51-51) and resurrection (28:2-4). Jesus has perfected the Law and the Prophets. At the death and resurrection of Jesus heaven and earth have passed away; one era has come to its perfection in Jesus; another is about to start (5:17-18).

The reaction of the disciples to the sight of Jesus is ambiguous. Some worship him. Matthew makes regular use of the verb "to worship" (Greek: *proskuneō*) to indicate the correct attitude of faith (see 2:2, 8 (!), 11; 8:2; 9:18; 14:33; 20:20; 28:9, 17). Some of the eleven demonstrate this faith in the risen Jesus. However, Matthew still reports: "but some doubted" (v. 17). The hesitation of the disciples in the presence of the risen Lord is one of the hallmarks of the synoptic resurrection accounts, each in its own way (see Mark 16:8 and Luke 24:10-11, 13-35, 36-37). It is even reported in the experience of Mary Magdalene and Thomas in the Gospel of John (John 20:11-17, 24-29). This theme continues to be an important part of Matthew's theology of the Church. All the Gospels have a realistic understanding and presentation of the disciples of Jesus. They believe, yet they falter in their belief. This situation of fragile belief is recorded across the Gospels because it retains its power in all experiences of post-Easter believers and missionaries. The presence of the risen Jesus, in whatever form, in the post-Easter Christian missionary experience, is never guaranteed unconditional acceptance of faith and subsequent action. There is always something of the "some who doubt" among us all.

Jesus opens his final instructions with a declaration about himself, and then spells out the consequences of such a declaration for his disciples and their mission. The man whom they had known as Jesus of Nazareth claims that all authority in heaven and on earth has been given to him (v. 18). The Jesus who had been crucified is now exalted to have power and authority over the whole of creation. This is nothing less than to claim that Jesus has taken over the authority and dignity that traditional Israel allowed only to Yhwh. Passages indicating this are innumerable. An example, and perhaps the most important Old Testament passage on the oneness of God and his complete authority, is found in Deuteronomy 6:4-9 which begins: "Hear, O Israel, the Lord our God, the Lord alone" (Deut 6:4). Behind Jesus' claim to absolute authority, there is probably also a reference to the giving of all authority to the "one like a son of man" in Daniel 7:14: "To him was given, dominion and glory and kingship, that all peoples, nations and languages should serve him." A careful reader of or listener to the Gospel of Matthew should not be surprised. Jesus has regularly promised that this would be the case, most recently in 26:64 when he announced to hostile Jewish leaders that the Son of Man would be exalted to the right hand of God (using words from Ps 110 and Dan 7:14). "The entire world was turned upside down by the resurrection of Jesus."[25]

On a mountain with his hesitant disciples, Jesus claims to have been given all the authority that, according to traditional Judaism, belonged to YHWH alone. Flowing from the uniqueness and universality of his authority, the Matthean Jesus breaks through three elements basic to Jewish belief and practice in vv. 19-20. There is a close logical link between Jesus' absolute authority, articulated in v. 18, and the commands that follow, generated by the expression "therefore." Only on the basis of his claims in v. 18 can Jesus *therefore* issue the commands that follow.

1. He commands his disciples to "Go therefore and make disciples of all nations" (v. 19a). They are to make "disciples." Matthew is almost the only New Testament author to use the verb "make disciples" (see 13:52; 27:57. See also, only Acts 14:21). He is also the evangelist who most frequently calls Jesus' disciples by the Greek expression for "disciple" (*mathētēs*) which means "one who engages in learning through instruction from another," across the Gospel story.[26]

---

[25] Luz, *Matthew*, 3:624.
[26] Danker, *A Greek-English Dictionary*, 609, s.v. *mathētēs*. See also Senior, *Matthew*, 346.

The eleven are "disciples," and have been learning from Jesus to this point. They are now to draw others into this circle of people who learn from Jesus, as v. 19 will indicate. Scholars have long debated whether Jesus' command to make disciples of "all nations" (Greek: *panta ta ethnē*) means "to all nations," including the nation of Israel, or "to all Gentiles," excluding Israel.[27] Ulrich Luz is most likely correct: "While it does not exclude a continuing mission to Israel, Matthew probably no longer had great hopes for it; that is shown by 22:8-10; 23:39–24:2 and 28:15. For him and his churches the separation of Israel into a majority hostile to Jesus and a minority consisting of disciples of Jesus is definitive."[28] Whatever one makes of that important debate, something astonishingly new in Jewish religious practice is commanded by Jesus. There had been openness to the idea of a universal salvation in the Prophets (see, for example, Isa 2:1-4). However, it had always meant a movement from the Gentile world toward Sion. There is only one people of God, with its Father Abraham, and its Law from Moses, the nation Israel. This is now rendered universal: the disciples, already a new people of God, founded by Jesus of Nazareth, are to "go out" to make disciples *of all nations*.[29]

---

27 In support of the former (majority) opinion, see John P. Meier, "Nations or Gentiles in Mt 28:19," *The Catholic Biblical Quarterly* 39 (1997): 94-102, and in support of the latter (minority) position, see Douglas R. Hare and Daniel Harrington, "'Make Disciples of all the Gentiles' (Mt 28:19)," in Daniel Harrington, *Light of All Nations. Essays on the Church in New Testament Research*, Good News Studies 3 (Wilmington, DE: Michael Glazier, 1982), 110-23.

28 Luz, *Matthew*, 3:631. See his excellent discussion of the debate on pp. 628-31.

29 See Davies and Allison, *Matthew*, 3:683: "The prophecy that in Abraham all the families of the earth will be blessed (Gen 12:3) comes to fulfilment in the mission of the Church."

2. The disciples are further instructed to "baptize" in the name of the Father and of the Son and of the Holy Spirit (v. 19b), thus introducing a new initiation rite for the new people of God, setting out on its mission. The Christian missionary is told to replace the initiation of circumcision with baptism. This interpretation of v. 19b depends upon the interpretation offered in this study of the theme of mission in the Gospel of Matthew. The systems of the Jewish Law (see 5:17-20) have now been overcome by the anticipated "end-time" of the death and resurrection of Jesus (27:51-54; 28:2-4). Neither Jews nor Gentiles who enter the Christian community generated by the missionaries that follow this injunction of the risen Jesus do so by means of circumcision. Such a situation must have been extremely difficult for many Matthean Christians, themselves Jewish Christians, and totally alien to their Jewish neighbors for whom circumcision was the sign of the uniqueness of the Jewish male.[30] But this was the radical nature of Christianity, and by the late 80s of the first century, as the Gospel of Matthew appeared, it is affirming its uniqueness. Baptism in the name of the Father, the Son and the Holy Spirit anticipates, but does not teach the doctrine of the Trinity, which came much later (at the Council of Nicea in 325 CE). As in Jesus' baptism the voice of the *Father* comes from heaven and the *Spirit of God* descends upon *Jesus* (3:16-17), the baptism practiced in the Matthean Church also recalled Father, Son, and

---

[30] It is sometimes pointed out that the practice of baptism in the early Church extended the initiation rite to women, as well as men. This is true, but hardly in the mind of Matthew at this point of his story of Jesus.

Holy Spirit, and most likely used a formula over the newly baptized that is recorded here.[31]

3. The final command broadens the basis of traditional Jewish faith, built upon the teaching and the learning of the Torah. It remained as the heart of the Jewish understanding of God's ways among his people and his people's approach to him. Jesus does not "replace" the Torah, but he "perfects" it (see 5:17-18). Jesus uses words commonly found in passages on the importance of the Torah: "to teach," "to observe," "commandments" (see, for example, Deut 5-6, esp. 6:1, where all these terms appear) to indicate a new teaching: "teaching them to observe all that I have commanded you" (v. 20a). No longer does the command to teach and observe look to the Torah, but to the teaching of Jesus. The Law of Moses has been perfected by the teaching of Jesus, but Jesus does not instruct his disciples to abandon the Law and replace it with the teaching of Jesus. However, from this point on, the Law will be interpreted through the teaching of Jesus. "Jesus not only was, he always is the 'only teacher' of his church (23:8). His proclamation makes the church's proclamation plain."[32]

But there is more to this final command. The teaching of Jesus that must be taught by the disciples is the teaching found in this

---

[31] See Luz, *Matthew* 3:632. For a fine discussion of the origins of Matthew's use of the expression, see Jane Schaberg, *The Father, the Son and the Holy Spirit. The Triadic Phrase in Matthew 28:19b*, Society of Biblical Literature Dissertation Series 61 (Chico, CA: Scholars Press, 1982). She argues that it is a development of the triad of the Ancient of Days, the one like a son of man and angels in Daniel 7. The use of the formula containing the names of Father, Son and Spirit is also found in Paul. See 1 Cor 6:11; 12:4-6; 2 Cor 13:13; Gal 4:6, and beyond: 1 Peter 1:2.

[32] Luz, *Matthew*, 3:633.

story of Jesus, especially as it has been magisterially expounded in his great discourses on the ethical organization of the community (5:1–7:29), on the mission and lifestyle of the disciples (10:1-42), on the nature of the kingdom (13:1-52), on the quality of life and care within the community (18:1-35), and on the end of time and the purpose of history (24:1–25:46).[33] These final words of the risen Jesus are a canonization of the Matthean Gospel, and it is quite possible that Matthew already understood himself as writing "Sacred Scripture." The development of a Christian Canon of Scripture was under way.[34]

Jesus' final words are not words of departure, but words assuring that he will always be with his disciples (v. 20b). These words point back to 1:23, where Jesus was promised as the Emmanuel, "God with us." The theme of the presence of Jesus has sounded across the entire story (see 9:15; 17:17; 18:20), with special intensity in the passion narrative (26:11, 18, 20, 23, 29, 36, 38, 40, 51, 69, 71). There are repeated stories of Jesus' helping presence among his disciples (see 8:23-27; 14:13-21, 22-23; 15:29-39; 17:1-8; 26:26-29). "Jesus' promise to be with his disciples to the end of the world again points back to the story of the earthly Jesus."[35]

In the Gospel of Luke the idea of ascension is a pictorial image of Jesus leaving this earth and returning to his Father, but in the Gospel of Matthew there is no trace of any such event. In fact, one could

---

[33] Some make an association between the mountain of the final appearance (20:16) and the mountain of the first discourse, the Sermon on the Mount (5:1) and claim this is what the disciples are to teach. It is better to look back to all of Jesus' teaching in the Gospel, especially if Jesus' five discourses have a symbolic connection with the five books of the Torah. See, for example, Meier, *Vision*, 45-51.

[34] See especially D. Moody Smith, "When Did the Gospels Become Scripture?" *Journal of Biblical Literature* 119 (2000): 3-20, especially pp. 7-18. On the development of the Christian Canon of Scripture, down to its definitive recognition by Athanasius in 367 CE, see Moloney, *Reading the New Testament*, 45-63.

[35] Luz, *Matthew*, 3:634.

say that the opposite is the case. Matthew's Gospel ends with Jesus' promise that he will never leave them. Of course, theologically, Luke is saying the same thing through his message of a return to the Father and his eventual sending of the Spirit. But whether it is Jesus' Spirit sent by the Father (Luke) or the abiding presence of Jesus who will never leave his Church (Matthew), the message of God's purposes to found and sustain a holy people in and through Jesus rings true.[36]

Although the story ends here, the reader knows what will take place after this concluding commission, thanks to Jesus' parable discourse (13:1-52) and his eschatological discourse (24:1–25:46). In these discourses Jesus told several parables which explained what would happen in the period between his resurrection and his return as the Son of Man at the close of the age. There will be periods of persecution when many will fall away (13:21). There will be a mixture of good and bad within the Church (13:24-30). Many will grow weary waiting for his return (25:1-13), but at the end of the age Jesus will come as the Son of Man to judge the nations (25:31-46). Thus the great commission (28:16-20) is not an ending but a beginning that invites the reader to discipleship and to the evangelization of the nations in the period between the death and resurrection of Jesus, the turning point of the ages, and the final coming of the Son of Man.

MISSION

The Law and the Prophets have been brought to their perfection. Thus, as risen Lord to whom all authority on earth and in heaven has been given, he can send his disciples to all nations, teaching what he taught them (28:16-20). This final missionary commission, sending the disciples to all the nations, does not stand in conflict with

---

[36] As Senior, *Matthew*, 348, puts it: "For Matthew ... the Risen Jesus himself is the equivalent to the divine presence within the community as it moves out into history."

Jesus' own life and ministry, but forms the culminating point of the Gospel's structure and message. The turning point of the ages takes place because of the death and resurrection of Jesus. His death and resurrection anticipate the end-time, and opens a new era in the life of the Christian community, but the traditional Jewish expectation of a final "day of the Lord" is still an important part of the Matthean historical and theological agenda (see especially 24:1–25:46). Jesus may have responded perfectly to God's design, and thus heaven and earth pass away, and all things are brought to their perfection (5:18). But much still lies ahead for his disciples.

For disciples of all ages, the heavens are still above, the earth is still firmly in place under their feet, and the end-time still lies somewhere in the unknown future! The crucified and risen Jesus will be with his community till the end of the age (28:20), but, sent by the Lord of heaven and earth (28:18), they are to carry out their mission in the in-between-time, in a bold new way that is different from their Jewish roots, until the end of the age (28:19-20). No doubt many of them were resisting this mission, preferring to stay with former, much-loved ways. This may be the reason for Matthew's placing such a powerful statement, sending his Christians out into mission, at the end of his story.[37] But it is not new. Their responsibilities have been made clear to them across the Gospel, as Jesus instructs them by both deed and word (see especially 8:1–11:30; 13:54–18:35).

In his final discourse, on the eve of his death and resurrection (24:1–25:6), Jesus instructs his disciples: "And this gospel of the kingdom will be preached throughout the whole world, as a testimony

---

[37] It has been argued that the warnings and the "woes" directed against the Pharisees found in 23:1-39 may also be directed toward the Matthean Christians who would like to return to their former life and practice in the synagogue across the road. The Pharisees were not reading or hearing Matthew 23, but Christians were. The passage is addressed to crowds and disciples in v. 1. Maybe there was the danger of a lurking "phariseeism" in many of them, as following Jesus was such a radical move from their former life.

to all nations; and then the end will come" (24:14). But none of this would have been possible if God had not acted decisively among us in the death and resurrection of Jesus. Matthew continues and develops the Pauline and Markan focus upon the transforming power of the resurrection, but he interprets it in his own way. The Church is living "the in-between time," gifted by the "turning point of the ages" through Jesus' death and resurrection. An essential aspect of the life of the Church is the proclamation of the Gospel of Jesus, making disciples of all nations until God's final gift that will come at the end of the age. He promises to be always with us in our missionary vocation (1:23; 28:20).

4

THE GOSPEL OF LUKE AND THE ACTS OF THE APOSTLES

Empowered by the Spirit, Witnesses to the Ends of the Earth (Luke 24:47-49; Acts 1:8)

On 1 June 2018, in his address to the national directors of the Pontifical Missionary Societies, Pope Francis challenged them: "Your regular book for prayer and meditation should be the Acts of the Apostles. Go there to find your inspiration. And the protagonist of that book is the Holy Spirit."[1] After some introductory reflections on the nature and story line of Luke and Acts, we will trace the intimate association that exists in Luke's thought between the Spirit and the mission of the Church.

The Acts of the Apostles is the "second volume" of a single work known as Luke-Acts. Some occasionally suggest that these two New

---

[1] The text is available at http://w2.vatican.va/content/francesco/en/speeches/2018/june/documents/papa-francesco_20180601_pontificie-opere-missionarie.html/. A more extended version of this chapter can be found in "The *Acts of the Apostles*: With the Spirit to the Ends of the Earth," in Fabrizio Meroni, ed., *Missio ad Gentes in the Acts of the Apostles*, Mission & Formation (Rome: Urbaniana University Press, 2019), 27-52.

Testament books may be from different hands.² But their prologues (Luke 1:1-4; Acts 1:1-2), the shared dedication to Theophilus, the explicit reference to two books in that dedication (Luke 1:3; Acts 1:1-2), and the many literary similarities between the two books make it clear that a single (and very skillful) author wrote a long and unified story. It recounts God's saving action from the preparation for the coming of Jesus in the Old Testament (Luke 1–2), to the bold preaching of the kingdom to the ends of the earth (Acts 28:23-31).³ Across the stories that announce and document Jesus' birth Luke presents figures from the Old Testament era who usher in the story of Jesus (Zechariah, Elizabeth, Joseph, Simeon, and Anna). John the Baptist, closely linked to these beginnings, also belongs to that era: "The law and the prophets were in effect until John came; since then the kingdom of God is proclaimed" (Luke 16:16). From those beginnings, the era of Jesus is told, highlighted by Jesus' initial journey from Nazareth (4:16-30) to his transfiguration on a mountain in Galilee, and its aftermath (9:28-50), followed by a further journey from Galilee to Jerusalem (9:51–19:44).

The city of Jerusalem becomes the fulcrum of God's sacred history. Jesus takes possession of its Temple, teaches there, and shares his final meal with the disciples. Jesus is arrested, crucified, and raised in Jerusalem.⁴ Unlike the accounts of Mark (16:7), Matthew (26:16-20), and John (21:1-25), the disciples do not return to Galilee. Jesus ascends to heaven from Jerusalem (Luke 19:45–24:52). Before ascending, he commissions his disciples to be witnesses of Jesus' message of repentance

---

2   See, for example, Mikael C. Parsons and Richard I. Pervo, *Rethinking the Unity of Luke and Acts* (Minneapolis: Fortress, 1993).

3   There are hints in Acts that Luke was aware of Paul's death (see Acts 20:22-25, 37-38; 21:11, 13), but he has chosen to ignore a tragic ending. It did not suit his purpose, as there is no place for pessimism in a story of an unstoppable Spirit-directed march from Jerusalem to Rome, and beyond.

4   On this, and especially the single "day" during which all the Easter events take place, from the discovery of the empty tomb till Jesus' ascension, see Moloney, *The Resurrection of the Messiah*, 69-99.

and forgiveness to the ends of the earth. But they are to remain in the city of Jerusalem "until you have been clothed with power from on high" (24:46-49). The Spirit-directed journey of Jesus closes in the city of Jerusalem as he returns to his Father. Already in these concluding moments of the Gospel story of Jesus, however, it becomes clear that another "era" will open with the mission of the apostles.

JESUS AND THE HOLY SPIRIT

Anticipating the theme of this chapter with its major focus upon the Acts of the Apostles, the story of the Spirit-driven journey from Jerusalem to the ends of the earth, the three eras of the Gospel of Luke depend upon the crucial and creative role that the Holy Spirit plays as each era opens.

- *The Spirit's role in preparing for the coming of Jesus.* The Spirit comes upon Mary in the annunciation of the forthcoming birth of Jesus (1:35). The Spirit overcomes Zechariah's dumbness, and he utters the *Benedictus* (1:67). Simeon, "guided by the Spirit" (2:25-27), comes to the Temple and takes the infant Jesus in his arms, announcing that the salvation for all peoples has come (vv. 29-32). John the Baptist announces that, unlike his baptism with water, Jesus will baptize "with the Holy Spirit and fire" (3:15-17).

- *The Spirit in Jesus' ministry.* In John's baptism the Spirit descends upon Jesus (3:31-32), leading him into the wilderness (4:1). In 4:14-30 Jesus begins his public ministry "filled with the power of the Spirit" (v. 14), announcing: "the Spirit of the Lord is upon me" (v. 18). The stage has been set for a Spirit-filled and Spirit-driven ministry of Jesus (see 10:20-21; 11:13;

12:10), until he hands over his Spirit to the Father in death (24:46).

- *The Spirit promised to the apostles.* The closing episodes of the Gospel and the opening passages in the Acts of the Apostles indicate a transition from one era to another. The promise of the gift of the Holy Spirit dominates these pages. In the Gospel, before he leaves the disciples on the day of the resurrection, Jesus promises the gift of the Spirit (24:46-49. See also 12:12). The disciples must stay in the city; there can be no return to Galilee for the Lukan view of God's saving presence. As the Acts of the Apostles opens, in Jerusalem the risen Jesus instructs his disciples: "You will be baptized with the Holy Spirit not many days from now" (Acts 1:5). The audience is aware that the Spirit who had directed Jesus' birth, ministry, and death will be "handed over" to the "witnesses."

THE ACTS OF THE APOSTLES

The book of Acts is a story of a journey that continues the journey of Jesus. Although Jesus is no longer physically present to his apostles, they are not on a "different" journey. The "power from on high" directs their journey, as it directed the journey of Jesus. However, it is another "era," designed by Luke to be open-ended so that the audiences of Luke-Acts can rightly claim that they belong to what might be called a "fourth era" of an ongoing journey beyond Rome "to the ends of the earth." That element of the inspired Lukan message on mission is not found *within the text*. For audiences across the Christian centuries it is *implied by the text*. Not active agents within the narrative of Luke-Acts, believing audiences are the fruit of the ongoing Spirit-filled missionary Church, exemplified by Paul as Acts closes: "proclaiming the kingdom of God and teaching about the Lord Jesus Christ with all boldness and without hindrance" (28:31).[5]

The narrative of Acts follows the founding apostles, beginning in Jerusalem, where the earliest community lives the idyllic experience of its first days, united in heart and mind, although not without failures (Acts 1:1–8:3). It gradually moves away from Jerusalem (8:4-40), until the conversion of Saul leads to further journeys that dominate the narrative: the journeys of Paul, establishing the Christian Church, again not without difficulties and failures, across the Mediterranean world (9:1–28:31). Luke's literary skills are evident in his description of Saul, the zealous persecutor of Christians in 7:58–8:3, as the Jerusalem section closes. After a brief interlude, during which the apostles make their first steps out of Jerusalem into Judea and Samaria (8:4-40), Saul, "still breathing threats and murder" returns to center stage, only to be "converted" in 9:1-19. An era dominated by his missionary activity begins.[6]

The Gospel of Luke and the Acts of the Apostles record three sacred "eras": the period of Old Testament preparation, the time of Jesus, and the time of the Christian Church.[7] As Jesus has traveled from Galilee to Jerusalem, the Church will reach out from Jerusalem to Rome (Acts 1:12–28:31). Only Mary, the mother of Jesus, plays a role

---

5 As Richard Pervo puts it, Acts is "an assurance that 'the ends of the earth' is not the arrival at a boundary, but realization of the limitless promises of the dominion of God" (cited by Mikeal C. Parsons, *Acts*, Paideia Commentaries on the New Testament [Grand Rapids: Baker Academic, 2008], 367). Written by a third-millennium Christian in Australia, the very existence of this chapter is proof of a Lukan audience that is fruit of Luke's Spirit-directed missionary journey "to the ends of the earth."

6 On Paul's so-called "conversion," see above pp. 5-9.

7 The recognition of these "eras" in Lukan thought owes much to the epoch-making study of Hans Conzelmann, *The Theology of St. Luke*, trans. Geoffrey Buswell (London: Faber & Faber, 1960). The title of the original German was *Die Mitte der Zeit*, identifying Jesus as the midpoint of history. Nowadays extensively criticized because of his identification of the characteristics of the "eras," Conzelmann uncovered an important feature of Luke's theological perspective.

in all three: before the birth of Jesus (Luke 1–2), during his ministry (Luke 8:19-21; 11:27-28), and in the early community in Jerusalem, after Jesus' death, resurrection, and ascension (Acts 1:12-14). Many memorable incidents are found in this exciting narrative: earthquakes (16:26), shipwrecks (27:41-44), avenging angels (12:23), harrowing escapes (9:23-25; 21:30-36); riots (19:23-41), murder plots (9:23; 23:12-15; 25:1-3), political intrigue (16:35-39; 22:24-29; 24:26-27), courtroom drama (23:1-10), and much more.[8] But undergirding this "story," full of journeys, encounters, successes, failures, and temporary setbacks, is a "discourse" about the action of God, through the steady intervention of the Holy Spirit in the life and mission of the apostles.[9]

Luke's dominant theological interest is to share his passionate conviction that the Holy Spirit drove the steady outreach of the "witnessing" to what God had done in and through Jesus. Those who "witnessed" the acts of Jesus become Jesus' "witnesses" to the ends of the earth. It begins in Jerusalem (1:8) and reaches the end of the earth (28:30-31), hinting that it must reach further. Luke wrote the Gospel and Acts to confirm and strengthen the belief of his Christians (see Luke 1:4).[10] This agenda for the narrative of the Acts of the Apostles was set as the Gospel closed. Jesus instructed the founding apostles: "Thus it is written, that the Christ should suffer and on the third day rise from the dead, and that repentance and forgiveness of sins should

---

[8] Mark Allan Powell, *Introducing the New Testament: A Historical, Theological, and Literary Survey* (Grand Rapids: Baker Academic, 2009), 191.

[9] The "story" is the way a narrative unfolds, moving chronologically from one event to another (with occasional flashbacks and hints of what lies ahead), the interaction among characters, along with all the adventures that mark the experience of the characters as time passes and a satisfactory conclusion emerges. The "discourse" is the author's motivation in writing the story that s/he wishes to communicate to an audience. In the case of New Testament narratives, authors did not simply wish to tell a story, but to convey a message about the action of God. On this, see Seymour Chatman, *Story and Discourse. Narrative Structure in Fiction and Film* (Ithaca, NY: Cornell University Press, 1978).

[10] Luke states this purpose explicitly in Luke 1:4, using a Greek word (*asphaleia*) to explain to Theophilus that he is writing that he "may have full confidence concerning the words in which you have been instructed" (AT). The word *asphaleia* is not about intellectual "truth," but "a mental state of certainty and security." See Luke T. Johnson, *The Gospel of Luke*, Sacra Pagina 3 (Collegeville: Liturgical Press, 1991), 28.

be preached in his name to all nations, beginning from Jerusalem. And behold, I send the promise of my Father upon you; but stay in the city until you are clothed with power from on high" (Luke 24:46-48).[11]

THE PROMISE OF THE SPIRIT

If the Gospel of Luke was a history of the Spirit-directed Jesus, then the Acts of the Apostles is a history of the Spirit-directed witness to Jesus by the founding apostles, especially Peter and Paul. The messenger, Jesus (the central figure in the Gospel), has become the subject of a message of what *must* happen for God's design to be fulfilled.[12] For this to happen, however, the Holy Spirit must come upon them (Acts 1:8a). The unstoppable urgency of the apostles' witness to what God has done in and through Jesus Christ, "to the ends of the earth," is directed by the Holy Spirit.

The command of Jesus in Acts 1:8b drives the structure of the narrative of Acts. The story begins with the disciples in Jerusalem, forging a link between the apostles and the risen Jesus.[13] He shares with them, promises a baptism with the Holy Spirit "not many days from now" (1:2-5). As they have no notion of their future mission, the apostles wonder when the end-time will come, and Jesus warns them

---

[11] Jesus foreshadows this promise during the journey of Jesus and the disciples to Jerusalem. He instructed them that in their future difficulties: "The Holy Spirit will teach you at that very hour what you are to say" (Luke 12:12).

[12] One of Luke's favorite words, in both the Gospel and the Acts, is the Greek expression *dei*. It means "must" or "it is necessary." It was necessary that Jesus die and rise from the dead (Luke 9:22; 13:33; 17:25; 24:7, 26; Acts 17:3), that Judas be replaced (Acts 1:22), that Paul visit Rome (Acts 19:21; 23:11; 25:10; 27:24), for the Gospel to be proclaimed to the Jews first (13:46), for the Christians to suffer tribulation and suffer for Christ's name (14:26; 9:16).

[13] An obvious historical "tension" exists between the ascension of Jesus reported in Luke 24:50-51, and its timing as after forty days' appearing to the apostles "speaking about the kingdom of God" (Acts 1:3). The number "forty" is most likely determined by the passing of fifty days between the Jewish feast of Passover (Jesus' death and resurrection) and Pentecost (the gift of the Spirit). This is part of Luke's plan to show the passing of time as God works in and through Jesus and his disciples. See Joseph A. Fitzmyer, "The Ascension of Christ and Pentecost," *Theological Studies* 45 (1984): 409-40.

against such useless thoughts. The periods of sacred history depend upon the Father (vv. 6-7). In v. 8 Jesus sets the agenda:

a) "You will receive power when the Holy Spirit has come upon you;

b) You will be my witnesses in Jerusalem, in all Judea and Samaria, and to the ends of the earth."

Jesus departs, but they ignore the commission that will take them from Jerusalem, into all Judea and Samaria, to the ends of the earth. After the description of Jesus' departure, creating a new situation where he was "out of their sight" (v. 9), the disciples stand dumbfounded, gazing into the clouds (v. 10), until two men in white robes tell them to move on.[14] Gazing into the sky will achieve nothing. They have a mission to complete in Jerusalem, all Judea and Samaria, and to the ends of the earth. Only when that mission is completed will Jesus return (v. 11).

Before setting out on the mission, however, the group of the Twelve must be reconstituted. Based upon Jesus' own choice of the Twelve (see 1 Cor 15:5; Mark 3:14) as a symbol of God's establishment of a new people, this group also serves Luke as the fundamental symbol of the vocation to be apostolic.[15] Unlike Mark (3:14) and Matthew (10:1), Luke tells his audience that Jesus appointed twelve, "whom he also named apostles" (Luke 6:13).[16] They are not only "disciples"

---

14 The "two men in white robes" in Acts 1:10 repeat the role of the "two men in dazzling clothes" who address the women at the empty tomb in Luke 24:4. On that occasion, in a fashion that parallels the instructions given to the apostles in Acts 1:11, the women are told that they are looking in the wrong place for "the living one," as they are in a place for the dead.

15 On the historical and theological significance of "the Twelve," as a group and as individuals, see the comprehensive study of Meier, *A Marginal Jew*, 3:125-285.

16 See Luke T. Johnson, *The Acts of the Apostles*, Sacra Pagina 5 (Collegeville: Liturgical Press, 1992), 38-40. Only Luke and Paul refer to the Twelve as "apostles." Paul regarded himself as an "apostle," even though he was not one of the Twelve (see especially 1 Cor 15:3-11; 2 Cor 10-12). The Greek word means "one sent out." Luke and Paul are especially concerned with the outreach of the Christian message and the Christian community "to the ends of the earth." The Lukan "Twelve Apostles" has become part of traditional Christian language. For Paul, it was possible to be an "apostle" without being one of the Twelve. The

who learn at the school of Jesus (Mark, Matthew, and John), but also apostles, sent out as witnesses to what they have learned.

Peter recalls the Spirit-filled inspiration of David's foretelling of the failure of one of that group (Acts 1:15-20). He asks the remaining eleven to seek the Lord's guidance so that the fundamental apostolic group to whom the power of the Most High has been promised might be re-constituted: "and the Lot fell on Matthias; and he was added to the eleven apostles" (vv. 21-26). Although not explicitly linked with an action of the Holy Spirit, whose words were uttered through David's mouth (v. 16), the casting of lots to choose between two fine witnesses to the ministry of Jesus (Barsabbas and Matthias) (v. 26) manifests that the Spirit of the Lord has intervened (see v. 24).

Based upon the promise of the Spirit and the missionary charge of 1:8, the directions of the two men dressed in white in 1:9-11, and the re-constitution of "the Twelve" in 1:12-26, the Spirit-directed mission of the Church unfolds as follows:

1. The gift of the Spirit of God and the mission in Jerusalem, under the leadership of Peter. This section closes with the presence of Saul the persecutor of Christians (2:1–8:3. See 1:8).

2. The mission spreads to all Judea and Samaria (8:4-40. See 1:8).

3. The zealot Saul, after an encounter with the risen Jesus, is baptized and filled with the Holy Spirit. Peter experiences the gift of the Spirit to the Gentile Cornelius. He consequently baptizes him, his household, and shares his hospitality (9:1–11:18).

---

title "The Acts of the Apostles" was added to this document late in the second century, but the "apostles" of Luke 6:12-16 are rarely mentioned (1:2; 4:36-37; 5:12; 8:1). The central figures are Peter and Paul, rather than the Twelve.

4. The Church at Antioch and the initial association between Paul and Barnabas generates what develops into Paul's mission "to the ends of the earth" (11:19–26:32. See 1:8).

5. The mission arrives at the center of the known world, Rome. Beginning in Jerusalem this brings the message to the far reaches of the earth. The missionary agenda of 1:8b is achieved because of the power of the Most High, promised in 1:8a (27:1–28:31).

Each of these unstoppable geographical steps, from Jerusalem, to all Judea and Samaria, and to the ends of the earth (v. 8b), is always a consequence of the intervention of God's Holy Spirit (v. 8a).

THE SPIRIT OF GOD AND THE MISSION IN JERUSALEM (ACTS 2:1–8:3)

The promises of Jesus (see Luke 24:46-49) come true in the dramatic events that take place "when the day of Pentecost had come" (Acts 2:1). The Spirit, "the promise of the Father" (see Luke 24:49; Acts 1:4), the "power from on high" (Luke 24:49), is given to the infant Church. The apostles break free of their fears (see Acts 1:12-14). Their transformation from fear to enthusiasm is so impressive that they are thought to be inebriated (see 2:13). They proclaim what God has done in and through Jesus (2:1-36), leading to sorrow, repentance and conversion from about 3000 on that first Pentecost day (v. 41). The first action of the Spirit-filled apostles in Acts fulfills Jesus' promise in Luke 24:47: "Repentance and forgiveness of sins is to be proclaimed."

The foundational nature of this event cannot be overestimated. Signs associated with the establishment of an original people of God at Sinai (see Exod 19:16-20: thunder, lightning and fire) return at this first Christian Pentecost (Acts 2:1-4).[17] The confusion of tongues that began at the Tower of Babel is overcome (see Gen 11:1-9), as people of many tongues and nations understand the disciples' words (Acts 2:5-12). "The parallelism (between the Old Testament episodes and Acts 2:1-4) fits the pattern of Luke's story: Jesus is the prophet who sums up all the promises and hopes of the people before him; in his apostolic successors, that promise and hope (now sealed by the Spirit) will be carried to all the nations of the earth."[18] This pattern of preaching that Jesus' mission, death and resurrection was part of God's plan, already foretold in the Old Testament, and the subsequent response of conversion and baptism, already established in Peter's Pentecost speech and its aftermath (2:14-42), is found across the many speeches in Acts.[19] A community attentive to the teaching of the disciples, breaking bread and praying together, with one heart and mind, emerges as the founding model of the future missionary community (vv. 42-47).[20]

The witnessing of the apostles and the Jerusalem community is related in 3:1–8:3. Highlighted by the power manifested in the apostles' preaching and healing in the city (3:1-26 [Peter and John at the Temple, and another speech from Peter], 4:1-37 [Peter and John

---

[17] The Jewish celebration of Pentecost (to this day) is the commemoration of the gift of the Law, the establishment of a covenant between God and a people, at Sinai, celebrated fifty days after Passover.

[18] Johnson, *Acts*, 47. First parenthesis added, second parenthesis original.

[19] This is the case, no matter who gives the speech. Comparisons between the speeches in Acts, no matter who delivers them (Peter, all the Jerusalem believers, Stephen, or Paul) show they are very similar. This does not mean that Luke "invented" everything, but he has certainly shaped all the speeches so that they correspond to his theological idea of Jesus as the fulfillment of God's will, already manifested in the Old Testament, and the need for everyone to have a change of heart, receive forgiveness and baptism. See Robert A. Spivey, D. Moody Smith, and C. Clifton Black, *Anatomy of the New Testament. A Guide to Its Structure and Meaning*, 7th ed. (Minneapolis: Fortress, 2013), 248-50, for a good summary.

[20] Luke will regularly insert summary statements about the unity and peace that existed in the Jerusalem community (see 1:14; 2:43-47; 4:32-37). This is Luke's way of indicating the ideal Christian community. His rhetoric suggests to readers: it was like this in the beginning, and thus should always be like this. But Luke does not hesitate to report serious failures (Ananias and Sapphira) and opposition (the apostles are persecuted, executed, and imprisoned), even in Jerusalem.

before the Council, and the response of the community in another speech], 5:1-42 [Ananias and Sapphira betray the community; signs and wonders are performed, the apostles are persecuted, closing with Gamaliel's warning that these men may be doing a work of God]). Luke wants his readers and hearers to recognize that Christianity emerged from the very heart of Israel: Jerusalem and its Temple. For Luke, God's design has not changed direction with the life, teaching, death and resurrection of Jesus that climaxed in Jerusalem, nor in the beginnings of the community witnessing to Jesus, that had its origins in Jerusalem. "Christianity emerged from Israel's very heart and is, therefore, the true expression of that ancient faith."[21]

A further turning point of the story is the problem of the "Hellenists" that leads to the appointment of seven men to serve them (6:1-7). The existence of Greek-speaking Hellenists and "the Hebrews" within the community is a first indication that the Gospel is reaching beyond its origins in the small group of frightened disciples of Jesus (see 1:1-14). The step into the choice of seven "deacons," chosen to serve the Hellenists, is necessarily marked by the presence of the Spirit. The whole community of disciples insists that the selection of these "men of good standing" must be based upon their being "full of the Spirit and of wisdom" (6:2-3). One of those servants, Stephen, is singled out: "a man full of faith and the Holy Spirit" (v. 5). They are delegated by means of an external sign that indicates the communication of the Spirit: prayer and the laying on of hands (v. 6).

Stephen, already described as full of the Holy Spirit (v. 5), takes center stage, manifesting the power and signs that accompany God's presence.[22] He may be one of the "servants," but his ministry of power

---

21 Spivey, Smith, and Black, *Anatomy*, 252.
22 The Greek word for "servant" is *diakonos*, and Catholic tradition has long looked back upon Acts 6 as the beginnings of a sacramental order called the diaconate. Stephen is often presented in Christian art in the vestments of an ordained deacon. Although there

indicates that he continues the mission of the foundational apostles. Falsely accused, he is arrested, and he delivers the longest speech in Acts (6:1–7:53). The speech does not deal with the charges against him, but by means of a long reflection on Israel's history, points to the past disobedience of the chosen people, questions the relevance of the Temple (see 7:47-50), and strongly denounces those who have betrayed and murdered Jesus (vv. 51-52). It closes: "You who received the law as delivered by angels and did not keep it" (v. 53). Whatever of the accusations of 6:11-14, he is condemned to death because of his "witness."[23] The theme of the Spirit, and the continuation of Jesus' ministry in the Spirit mark his death. He prays as Jesus prayed: "Lord Jesus, receive my spirit" (7:59; see Luke 23:46), and "Lord, do not hold this sin against them" (Acts 7:60; see Luke 23:34). Those who die for Christ repeat the death of Christ.[24] As the episode closes, the reader is introduced to the hero of the second half of Acts: "And Saul was consenting to his death" (Acts 8:1a. See 7:58). The hero of the latter parts of the Acts of the Apostles has been introduced, however enigmatically.

THE MISSION TO ALL JUDEA AND SAMARIA (8:4-40)

The fruits of martyrdom are reported in 8:4-40. The Christians scatter as Saul persecutes them, proclaiming the word as they scatter (8:1b-3). Scattering believers leads to an expanding Christian witness. Philip makes converts in Samaria, including "Simon who had previously

---

were certainly appointed people who had a ministry of "service" in the early Church (see as early as Rom 16:1; Phil 1:1; Eph 6:21; 1 Tim 3:8), the sacramental order appeared much later.

23 Parsons, *Acts*, 108: "Stephen is not pitting Christianity over against Judaism; rather he is aligning himself and his group with what he considers to be the 'best' in Jewish history" (p. 108).

24 See Johnson, *Acts*, 142-44. Here, and throughout his commentary, Johnson rightly points out that the apostles are not only "witnesses," but continue Jesus' "prophetic" presence.

practiced magic" (vv. 4-13. See vv. 9-13), but the report of the wondrous events of Philip's ministry is interrupted by a description of the mission of Peter and John to those who had already accepted the word in Samaria. The narrative has reached a turning point, as the apostles move on from Jerusalem to bear witness in all Judea and Samaria as the risen Jesus had promised in 1:8. Peter and John pray that – as they have already received the Spirit in Jerusalem – those Samaritans who were baptized in the name of Jesus Christ might also receive the Holy Spirit (v. 15). God answers their prayer: they lay hands upon the baptized Samaritans, and they receive the Spirit (v. 17). The report of the brief encounter between the apostles and Simon the magician is not primarily interested in the historical figure of Simon,[25] but on the insistence of the apostles Peter and John that nothing can "purchase" the Spirit. It is "God's gift" (vv. 18-25. See v. 20). Only tragedy can follow those who think they can control the action of God by their worldly skill and financial means.

An angel of the Lord directs Philip to continue his movement away from Jerusalem "toward the south to the road that goes down from Jerusalem to Gaza" (v. 26). The well-known encounter between Philip and the Ethiopian eunuch on that road south takes place through the intervention of the Spirit: "The Spirit said to Philip, 'Go over to this chariot and join it'" (v. 29). After having the Scriptures explained by the Spirit-directed Philip, the non-Jewish eunuch is baptized (vv. 27-38). "When he came up out of the water, the Spirit of the Lord snatched Philip away" so that he might continue his mission in all Judea, passing through Azotus, all the region and all the towns, until he reached Caesarea (v. 40).[26]

---

[25] Over the centuries, there has been much speculation about the relationship between the Simon the magician of Acts 8:9-25 and the figure of the proto-Gnostic Simon Magus. For a summary of this speculation, see Joseph A. Fitzmyer, *The Acts of the Apostles*, The Anchor Bible 31 (New York: Doubleday, 1998), 403-4.

[26] Azotus is another name for the southern port city of Ashdod (see 1 Macc 9:15). Philip's

The section of the narrative that deals with the second stage in Jesus' promised commissioning of his apostles to bear witness in all Judea and Samaria (1:8) is relatively brief. Their presence in Jerusalem (2:1–8:3), the "Pentecost of the Gentiles" in Peter's baptism of the Roman Cornelius, and its aftermath (9:1–11:18), Paul's mission to the ends of the earth (11:19–26:30), and his preaching in Rome (26:30–28:31) are longer in the telling. Nevertheless, like other turning points in the fulfillment of the commission of 1:8b, they are dominated by the theme of the gift of the Holy Spirit (1:8a. See vv. 14-17, 19-21, 39).

PETER (AND PAUL) REACH OUT TO THE GENTILE WORLD (9:1–11:18)

The next stage in God's plan to take the Gospel to the ends of the earth is prepared in the well-known account of Paul's conversion (9:1-22). The encounter with the risen Jesus on the Damascus road, his time with Ananias in Damascus, and his preaching there, which "confounded the Jews who lived in Damascus" (9:22) are recorded on two further occasions in Acts (see 22:3-21; 26:12-18).[27] Luke shapes this account around two major moments. The first is Paul's dramatic encounter with the risen Jesus (9:1-9). The second is his sojourn with Ananias in Damascus (vv. 10-19). During the latter, the Lord described Paul's future mission: "Go, for he is an instrument whom I have chosen to bring my name before Gentiles and kings and before the people of Israel" (v. 15). Before this mission can begin, as with all other major turning points in Luke's story, Ananias "laid his hands on Saul and said, 'Brother Saul, the Lord Jesus who appeared to you on your way here, has sent me so that you may regain your sight and be filled with the Holy Spirit" (v. 17).

---

contact points are on the road south, to Gaza, Azotus (farther north on the coast), all the towns, finally arriving in the northern port city of Caesarea Maritima. The geography matches the commission of 1:8 (all Judea).

27 On the threefold telling of Paul's conversion, see Johnson, *Acts*, 170.

After initial witnessing in Damascus, hunted by some Jewish people, he escapes, and returns to Jerusalem, the cradle of Christianity (vv. 19b-30). From there, he is sent home to Tarsus (v. 30). The Lukan comment of v. 31 indicates that the agenda set by the commission of 1:8 is drawing to a close: "Meanwhile the church throughout Judea, Galilee, and Samaria had peace and was built up. Living in the fear of the Lord and the comfort of the Holy Spirit, it increased in numbers." Paul, who will follow the leadership of Peter to become the hero of the mission to the ends of the earth (11:19–26:30), has entered the narrative. He disappears in 9:30, but will return in 13:1-3. In the meantime (9:32–11:18), Peter takes center stage in a further Spirit-filled turning point in the earliest Church's mission.

Peter works wonders in the name of Jesus Christ (9:32-35: the healing of Aeneas; vv. 36-42: the raising of Tabitha/Dorcas). Most importantly, he is the key figure in the explicit acceptance of the mission to the Gentiles through the baptism of the Roman centurion, Cornelius (10:1–11:18). It is a complex, and somewhat repetitious account. Cornelius has a vision at Caesarea, at this stage the frontier of the Gospel's outreach (see 8:40), instructing him to summon Peter from Joppa (10:1-9a). Simultaneously Peter has a vision, insisting that what has once been regarded as "unclean" can no longer be so, as God has made all things clean (vv. 9b-16). The Spirit instructs a puzzled Peter that he must go to meet the men from Cornelius, who has had a vision of a holy angel, sending for Peter (vv. 17-23). Cornelius' servants bring Peter to Caesarea, where they have a moving encounter (vv. 17-29). Cornelius tells Peter of his vision (vv. 30-33).

Peter's response is a missionary speech (vv. 34-43), dominated by the theme of his opening words: "Truly I perceive that God shows no partiality, but in every nation anyone who fears him and does what is right is acceptable to him" (vv. 34-35). Luke's Spirit-filled missionary agenda is stated. Peter tells Cornelius about Jesus, "anointed with the

Holy Spirit and with power" (AT), his ministry, death and resurrection, and the role of the apostles as his witnesses. "We are witnesses to all that he did both in Judea and Jerusalem. ... He commanded us to preach to the people" (vv. 41-42). As Peter ends his words, *before* anything else happens "the Holy Spirit fell upon all who had heard the word" (v. 44). All are amazed "that the gift of the Holy Spirit had been poured out even on the Gentiles" (v. 45). The same phenomena that accompanied the pouring out of the Spirit at Pentecost reappear: "They heard them speaking in tongues and extolling God" (v. 46. See 2:5-11). As a *consequence* of the gift of the Holy Spirit, Peter baptizes Cornelius and his company (vv. 44-48). "The gift of the Holy Spirit has been poured out even on the Gentiles" (v. 45). The speech opened insisting that "God shows no partiality," and closes asking a question that requires a negative response: "Can anyone withhold the water for baptizing these people who have received the Holy Spirit just as we have?" (v. 47).[28]

Peter returns to Jerusalem where he is criticized by the circumcision party. He should not have gone to an uncircumcised man and eaten with him. In response, Peter retells all the events that took place in Caesarea (11:1-18). He repeats the news of the action of the Spirit in the coming of the messengers (v. 12), and the descent of the Spirit as he spoke to Cornelius and his household (v. 15). He concludes by recalling a promise of Jesus: "John baptized with water, but you will be baptized with the Holy Spirit" (v. 16), insisting that God's gift of the Spirit to the Jewish disciples is now available to the Gentiles (v. 17). Peter's report meets no opposition. It is received in silence as they glorify God, saying "Then to the Gentiles also God has granted

---

[28] The Greek expression that generates the question (*mēti*) is rhetorical. It demands a negative response. See Friedrich A. Blass, Albert Debrunner, and Robert W. Funk, *A Greek Grammar of the New Testament and Other Early Christian Literature* (Chicago: Chicago University Press, 1961), 226, §440.

repentance unto life" (v. 18).²⁹ Even though Peter's Jerusalem speech in 11:1-18 repeats what has happened in Caesarea, it accentuates the theological importance of this moment: "If then God gave the same gift to them as he gave to us when we believed in the Lord Jesus Christ, who was I that could withstand God?" (v. 17). God is the absent, but ever-central character in Acts, shaping the lives of people and communities through the gift of the Holy Spirit. Peter will return to this moment in his defense of the Gentile mission at the so-called Jerusalem Council (see 15:7-9).

THE MISSION "TO THE ENDS OF THE EARTH" (11:19–26:32)

A series of episodes report the continued spread of the Gospel, as opposition is vanquished (11:19–12:25). Stephen's mission as far as Phoenicia and Cyprus has produced converts who come to Antioch, preaching the Lord. The field is ripe for harvesting, so Luke introduces Barnabas, another key figure at a turning point of the narrative. Described as "a good man, full of the Holy Spirit and faith" (11:24), he goes from Antioch to Tarsus, seeking out Saul. It is at Antioch that "the disciples were for the first time called Christians" (11:26). The disciples, warned by the Spirit through a prophet named Agabus that suffering is near at hand determine to bring goodness to all who are suffering in Judea, through the ministry of Barnabas and Saul (11:27-30). Adventure, misadventure, and God's presence continues as Herod executes James and puts Peter in prison (12:1-5), but Peter is miraculously released (vv. 6-19). Herod, who has no interest in the sufferings of the people of Tyre and Sidon (contrast the attitude of the

---

29   This is one of many occasions in Acts where Luke writes an account to show that God's plan will brook no failure or opposition. We are aware from other early Christian literature, especially Paul's Letter to the Galatians, that the passage into the Gentile world - especially the question of circumcision - was conflicted, and that even Peter (and Barnabas) were ambiguous about it (see Gal 2:11-14).

Christians to the poor in Judea in 11:27-30), is smitten by "an angel of the Lord" and dies ignominiously (12:20-23). The word of God "continued to advance" as Barnabas, Saul, and John Mark return to Jerusalem (vv. 24-25).

The scene is set for the fourth major section of the narrative, determined by the commission and the promise of the Spirit in 1:8. In the Gospel of Luke, Jesus journeyed from Nazareth in Galilee, through Jerusalem, to his Father. In the Acts of the Apostles, the apostles witness to the good news *about* Jesus through Cyprus and Asia Minor (first missionary journey: 13:1–14:28), into Macedonia (second missionary journey: 15:36–18:22), consolidated in Ephesus and Greece (third missionary journey: 18:23–21:14). Jerusalem is not forgotten. The only interruption to this triumphant march from Jerusalem to Ephesus, Athens and Corinth is the Council of Jerusalem. After the success of the first formal mission to the Gentiles (13:1–14:28), the Church gathers to assess whether or not this mission is part of God's plan (15:1-35). Jerusalem, the fulcrum of God's saving history, remains an essential point of reference for a movement that has its roots in God's promises to Israel.

Before this major journey begins, the Holy Spirit again intervenes. As the Church in Antioch is at prayer, "the Holy Spirit said, 'Set apart for me Barnabas and Saul for the work to which I have called them'" (13:2). "Sent out by the Holy Spirit" (v. 4) the first missionary journey begins. At Paphos in Cyprus they meet opposition from a Jewish false prophet. "Filled with the Holy Spirit," Paul strikes him blind, and the proconsul, Sergius Paulus believes (vv. 4-12. See v. 9). From Cyprus they arrive in Asia Minor at Perga. Asked to preach in the synagogue, Paul speaks as an Israelite to Israelites. Regularly across this section of Acts, Paul tries to show that Jesus Christ is the fulfillment of Jewish hopes (13:16-41). Some hear the message; others reject it (vv. 42-43). Rejection leads him to go to the Gentiles (vv. 44-49). The first stage of the missionary journey, however, fills the disciples "with joy and the Holy Spirit" (v. 52). Similar missionary activities and responses continue in Iconium, Lystra, Derbe, and they return to Antioch via Iconium, Pamphilia, Perga, and Attalia (14:1-26). Despite the regular rejection and misunderstanding they have experienced, the apostles are able to relate "all that God had done and how he had opened a door of faith for the Gentiles" (v. 27).

The missionary journeys are put on hold, as a group of Christians from Judea insist that circumcision is essential for admission to their ranks (15:1-5). Another critical moment in the narrative emerges, and it is again dominated by the action of the Holy Spirit. The so-called Council of Jerusalem opens with the intervention of Peter (vv. 6-11). He recalls his initiating role among the Gentiles: "And God, who knows the human heart, testified to them by giving them the Holy Spirit, just as he did to us; and in cleansing their hearts by faith he has made no distinction between them and us" (vv. 8-9). He receives the support of the equally foundational figure of James (vv. 15-21). A decision is made in favor of Paul and Barnabas. A letter is sent insisting that circumcision is not required (vv. 22-29), because "it has seemed good to the Holy Spirit and to us to impose on you no further burden than these essentials" (15:28).

After a dispute over the role of John Mark, who had abandoned the first missionary journey (see 13:13), Paul and Barnabas separate. Paul attempts to resume his mission in Asia Minor, taking Silas with him (15:36–16:5). In a strange intervention, the Holy Spirit leads Paul across Asia Minor, into Macedonia. In fact, Paul and his companions are not active as they cross Phrygia and Galatia, "having been forbidden by the Holy Spirit to speak a word in Asia" (16:6). His journey takes him farther west, to Troas, the seaport on the western coast of Asia Minor that provides immediate access to Macedonia and Greece. During the night a vision provides a reason for this prohibition. They are being driven elsewhere by the Spirit: a man of Macedonia appears in a dream saying "Come over to Macedonia and help us" (v. 9).

Paul arrives in Philippi, via the port of Neapolis where he is immediately successful in his conversion of Lydia (16:6-15).[30] But his saving and curing presence to a possessed slave girl leads to his imprisonment, accused by the girl's angry owners. As is now a familiar pattern, Paul is miraculously freed; the doors are opened and he baptizes his repentant jailer (vv. 16-34). Subsequent discussion over the treatment of Paul and his companions leads to Paul's first indication to his oppressors that he is a Roman citizen. He receives the apologies of the authorities, visits Lydia, and leaves to continue their mission (vv. 35-40). Passage and preaching in Thessalonica and Beroea leads to the usual mixed response (17:1-15). From here Paul journeys to Athens, where he not only uses his initial approach to the Jews, but also confronts the pagan culture and religion of the city. Set in the heart of Greek culture and religion, this passage is highlighted by Paul's speech on the Areopagus, a central point for public speech in Athens. Paul's speech does not use the Hebrew Scriptures, but cites Greek authorities (the poet Aratus) to point them to the unknown God, a man who has been raised from the dead.[31] As always, the response is mixed: "Some mocked; but others said 'We will hear you again about this'" (vv. 16-34. See v. 32).

A parallel narrative pattern and theological message shapes Paul's ongoing journey through Corinth, where his rejection by the Jews

---

30 Across Acts there are a number of reports where the author uses "we." They begin at Troas, and are regularly (but not always) associated with sea voyages (see 16:10-17; 20:5-15; 21:1-18; 27:1-28:16). For many, this shows the presence of the author of Acts, and thus an indication of a first-hand witness to the events reported, and evidence of the historical reliability of Acts. Not all agree. For a balanced study of the "we-passages," see Brown, *An Introduction*, 322-27.

31 In Athens the death of Jesus is not mentioned, only Jesus' being raised from the dead.

leads to a definitive choice: "From now on I will go to the Gentiles" (18:7). But even here he meets conflict, and is eventually led to the Roman authorities by his Jewish enemies. Gallio, the Roman Proconsul of Achaia, dismisses them (18:1-17). Paul brings his second missionary journey to an end as he returns, via Cenchreae (the port of Corinth), Ephesus, from where he sets sail, and Jerusalem, to the community in Antioch. While in Ephesus, he promises the Jews that he will return, if God so wills (vv. 18-22).[32]

The third journey begins immediately. After initiating the final missionary journey in Galatia and Phrygia (18:23), Paul dedicates himself to a long and trouble-filled experience in Ephesus (18:24–19:41). The enigmatic figure of Apollos appears briefly (18:24-28. See further, 1 Cor 1:12; 3:4-6). Coming to Ephesus this eloquent Alexandrian preaches the "way of the Lord" and "the things concerning Jesus" with skill and passion (v. 6). But "he only knew the baptism of John." No explicit mention is made of the Spirit, but his baptism is defective. This is corrected by Priscilla and Aquila. He is thus able to travel to Achaia and be welcomed among the brethren in Corinth (see 19:1), showing that "the Messiah is Jesus" (v. 28). Apollos serves as a model for the situation that Paul himself finds in Ephesus while Apollos is in Corinth (19:1-7). Some believers only know of the baptism of John. After due instruction, they are baptized in the name of the Lord Jesus. "When Paul laid hands on them, the Holy Spirit came upon them" (v. 6). The third missionary journey opens in Ephesus with two visible experiences of the power of the Holy Spirit, transforming Apollos and others in Ephesus who only knew the baptism of John.

---

[32] The reference to Gallio as the Proconsul of Achaia is one of the fixed points for determining a chronology for Paul. There is archeological evidence (an inscription found in Delphi) that Gallio was the Proconsul some time across 51-52 CE. See Jerome Murphy-O'Connor, *St. Paul's Corinth. Texts and Archaeology*, Good News Studies 6 (Wilmington, DE: Michael Glazier, 1983), 141-52. See Spivey, Smith, and Black, *Anatomy*, 277, for a fine photograph of the inscription.

In Ephesus Paul preaches boldly in the face of many obstacles, but his journey to the ends of the earth intrudes. While in Ephesus, "Paul resolved in the Spirit to go through Macedonia and Achaia, and then go on to Jerusalem. He said 'After I have gone there I must also see Rome'" (v. 21). The audience, hearing Paul's Spirit-filled decision, are aware that he will indeed journey to Rome, and Luke's account of his mission will end there.

Paul's preaching against false gods leads to the riot initiated by the silversmiths who see that Paul's words brings their trade to an end. After a resounding encounter between the worshipers of Artemis and Paul (vv. 34-41), Paul leaves Ephesus with the problem unresolved. He journeys through some of his earlier mission fields (20:1-6). Returning to Asia Minor he preaches at such great length at Troas that a young man sitting in a window falls to sleep and crashes to his death, but Paul restores him. Nothing can stop the spread of God's word (vv. 7-12).

In a fashion that matches many "farewell speeches" found in both biblical and classical literature, Paul sails from Troas to Jerusalem, stopping at Miletus so that he could address the leaders of the Church from Ephesus, assembled there (20:1-38). It is a moving speech, full of emotion and affection, and a commissioning that they persevere in their faith and mission.[33] Paul looks back to what has been achieved, and courageously ahead to all that God may have in store for him. At the heart of his discourse, Paul indicates that everything that has happened and will happen is the result of the active presence of the Holy Spirit: "And now, as a captive to the Spirit, I am on my way Jerusalem, not knowing what will happen to me there, except that the Holy Spirit testifies to me in every city that imprisonment and

---

[33] For a study of farewell testaments, see William Kurz, *Farewell Addresses in the New Testament*, Zacchaeus Studies: New Testament (Wilmington, DE: Michael Glazier, 1990). See also Johnson, *Acts*, 359-68.

persecutions are waiting for me" (20:22-23). He travels directly to Jerusalem (21:1-14). This is the first time that Paul's journeys have not returned to his home-Church of Antioch. The God-directed cycle of Jerusalem to Rome must be accomplished (see 1:8). As he farewells a dedicated group in Caesarea, before the final leg of his journey to Jerusalem, he tells them, in a way that renders more explicit what he said at Miletus: "For I am ready not only to be bound but even to die in Jerusalem for the name of the Lord Jesus" (21:13). The narrative stage is set for the final journey: the word of the Lord will make its final journey from Jerusalem to Rome (see 1:8).

The voyage toward Jerusalem is governed by the Spirit who halts Paul's travels at Tyre for seven days, until the Spirit allows Paul and his company to resume the journey through Ptolemais to Caesarea (see 21:4). There the prophet Agabus takes Paul's belt, binds his feet and hands with it, announcing: "Thus says the Holy Spirit, 'This is the way the Jews in Jerusalem will bind the man who owns this belt and will hand him over to the Gentiles'" (21:11).

On arrival in Jerusalem, Paul visits James, the leader of the Jerusalem community, and shares with him the success of the Gentile mission. He is able to announce that what was decided at the Jerusalem Council in 15:1-29 has been put into effect among those received into Christianity without circumcision (21:15-26). Immediately following this episode, however, Jews from Asia, aware of Paul's work among the uncircumcised, create a disturbance in the Temple, accusing Paul of "teaching men everywhere against the people and the law and this place; moreover he has also brought Greeks into the Temple, and he has defiled this holy place" (v. 28). Roman authorities arrest Paul (vv. 27-36). From this point on the narrative is made up of a series of encounters between Paul and Roman authorities where Paul must answer the accusations of his Jewish enemies.

He defends himself in Jerusalem as a "citizen of no mean city" (v. 39),[34] reporting the account of his conversion and his mission to the Gentiles (21:37–23:21). None of this is of interest to the Romans. Discovering he is a Roman citizen, they send him back to the Jewish Council (vv. 22-29). His Jewish credentials impress some, but not others, and that night "the Lord stood by him and said, 'Take courage, for as you have testified about me at Jerusalem, so must you bear witness also at Rome'" (22:30–23:11. See v. 11). As Paul's opponents concoct a plot to murder him, "the son of Paul's sister" (v. 16) hears of it, informs Paul, held in the Roman barracks, and he is swept away by the authorities to the Governor Felix in Caesarea, the seat of Roman authority in Palestine (23:12-35).

From now on a series of different trials take place, at Caesarea, before Felix (24:1-27), Porcius Festus (25:1-12), King Agrippa and his wife Bernice (25:13–26:32). Paul fulfills the destiny promised by Jesus to his disciples: "And you will be brought before kings and governors in my name" (Luke 21:12). At each trial Paul's defense is the same: he has done nothing to discredit the traditions of Israel, as he has been singled out by an act of the God of Israel to proclaim the saving effects of the death and resurrection of Jesus. "To this day I have had the help that comes from God, and so I stand here testifying both to small and great, saying nothing but what the prophets and Moses said would come to pass: that the Christ must suffer, and that, by being the first to rise from the dead, he would proclaim light both to the people and to the Gentiles" (Acts 26:22-23. See Luke 2:31-32; 24:25-27, 44-46). At each stage across these trials, Paul is declared innocent (23:29; 25:25; 26:31-32). It is as an innocent witness to the truth (like Jesus in the Lukan passion narrative [see especially Luke 23:47]), that Paul sails for Rome (Acts 27:1).

---

34 He is from the city Tarsus, and thus a Roman citizen.

ROME: THE CENTER OF THE KNOWN WORLD (27:1–28:31)

The perilous sea journey, described as Luke's "literary *tour de force*,"[35] is reported in 27:1–28:10. After an initial easy journey at the right time of the year (27:1-8), a decision is made – against Paul's advice – to continue the journey in the winter (vv. 9-12). From that point on every possible peril is faced: storm at sea (vv. 13-20), starvation (vv. 21-25), and possible shipwreck (vv. 26-32). Paul advises correctly in every situation, and even miraculously provides food for everyone as they are starving (vv. 33-38). They come to land in Malta, where they experience dangers (28:3-6: the episode with the viper), again overcome by Paul. They are made welcome by the local people (27:39–28:10). They take ship in Malta, and finally "came to Rome" (28:11-16. See v. 16). As throughout Acts, the Christian community, Peter and Paul continually face danger and opposition, but it is overcome by the power of their miraculous activity and the persuasion of their proclamation of the Gospel.

In Rome, Paul tells his story of trial, and is asked to explain himself to the local authorities. As always, some believe, and some reject what Paul has to tell them (vv. 17-25a). Acts closes with Paul's final use of Israel's Scriptures to legitimate his message and his turning away from Israel as the fulfillment of the promise of the Holy Spirit made through the Prophet Isaiah: "The Holy Spirit was right" (v. 25b). "Let it be known to you then that this salvation of God has been sent to the Gentiles; they will listen" (v. 28). Paul's mission to the Jews has come to a close, and from Rome the Gospel will be preached to the Gentiles. Luke tells of the relentless and unstoppable proclamation of the message of what God had done in and through Jesus. His second

---

[35] See Johnson, *Acts*, 450.

volume closes with the information that Paul remains in Rome for two years, courageously and openly "proclaiming the kingdom of God and teaching about the Lord Jesus Christ" (vv. 30-31). Spirit-filled Christian witness has not arrived at a boundary, but at a promise of a future.

MISSION

The commissions of Jesus in Luke 24:46-49 and Acts 1:8 have been fulfilled, thanks to the never-failing presence of the Holy Spirit who empowers and directs his apostles, especially Peter and Paul, to take the Gospel from Jerusalem to the ends of the earth. Opposition emerges from the Jews who will not accept an uncircumcised Christian, and from the Romans, who cannot understand what Paul represents, and do not want to know. Even the elements, storms, starvation, and shipwreck threaten this journey from Jerusalem to Rome. All opposition fails. Accompanied by signs and wonders that manifest the guiding presence of the Holy Spirit, the apostles' witness to the kingdom reaches out to the ends of the earth (see Luke 24:46-49; Acts 1:8).

Pope Francis claimed that the Holy Spirit is the protagonist of the Acts of the Apostles. A close reading of the narrative indicates that he is correct:

- The promise of the Holy Spirit (1:5, 8).
- The Holy Spirit reconstitutes the Twelve (1:15-20).
- The Holy Spirit comes upon the disciples at Pentecost (2:1-36).
- The Holy Spirit inspires the mission dedicated to the Greek-speaking people in Jerusalem (6:1-7).
- Stephen hands over his Spirit in martyrdom (7:59).

- The Holy Spirit directs the Samaritan mission (8:15-25).

- The Holy Spirit leads Philip to instruct and baptize the Ethiopian eunuch (8:29), and snatches him away on further mission (8:40).

- The gift of the Holy Spirit brings Saul's conversion to conclusion (9:1-17).

- The Holy Spirit descends upon Cornelius and his household (10:1-11:18).

- The Holy Spirit singles out Barnabas and Paul for the Gentile mission (13:1-4; 15:8-9).

- The Holy Spirit inspires the decisions of the Jerusalem Council (15:8, 28, 29).

- The Holy Spirit directs Paul from Asia to Macedonia (16:6-9).

- Apollos and believers in Ephesus who know Jesus and the baptism of John are baptized into the Holy Spirit (18:24-28; 19:19:1-6).

- The Holy Spirit reveals Paul's destiny (19:21; 20:22-23; 21:11, 13).

- Paul's final return to Jerusalem is directed by the Holy Spirit (21:4).

- Finally in Rome, Paul declares: "the Spirit is right" (28:25).

God, through the intervention of the Holy Spirit, is in control of history, and guides his "apostles" of all ages through their difficulties, sinfulness and rejection. A third generation Christian (see Luke 1:1-4),

Luke was aware of ambiguities in his experience of Church. But Luke wants to proclaim to individuals and communities that, guided by the Holy Spirit, miracles *can happen*. God's outreach to the ends of the earth *can be successful*. Our own experience of a fragile Church is an indication that, despite failure, the Gospel reaches out to the ends of the earth. Luke asks Christians, witnessing at the ends of the earth, to accept Luke's view of *how things should be* in God's Church. The call to mission continues, the Holy Spirit is present, and the saving power of God can be found.

Luke's two volumes call Christians *to be missionaries, witnesses* whose testimony fills the pages of a living *third volume*, telling what God and the Holy Spirit have done for us in and through Jesus Christ.

5

THE GOSPEL OF JOHN

The Foundation of the Church and Its Mission: "'It is finished.' Then he bowed his head and handed down the Spirit" (John 19:30)

The narrative world of the Fourth Gospel is unlike anything else in the New Testament. John's originality is spectacularly present in the questions that concern us: the foundation of the Church and its mission. In different ways, Paul, Mark, Matthew, and Luke locate the foundation of the Christian mission in "the power of the resurrection" (Phil 3:10). John continues this tradition, but develops it further, drawing the foundation of the Church into his theology of the Cross (John 19:16b-37), and the beginnings of the mission in the command of the risen Jesus (20:21). The mission of Jesus determines the mission of the disciples. Jesus is the sent one of the Father who makes God known in his loving self-gift (see 3:16-17; 4:34; 17:1-19). He asks his disciples to continue that revealing love in the time between his departure and return (13:34-35; 15:12, 17; 17:21-26), and to abide in him (esp. 15:1-11).[1]

THE FOUNDATION OF THE CHURCH: JOHN 19:16b-37

A New Family at the Cross

Following the trial of Jesus by Pilate, dominated by the theme of Jesus' kingship (18:28–19:16a), five brief scenes report Jesus' crucifixion.[2] He is summarily crucified, but Pilate continues to insist, in Hebrew, Greek and Latin, that this man was King of the Jews. The chief priests reject this claim, but Pilate insists it must remain (19:16b-22). At the Cross, the soldiers decide not to tear apart Jesus' seamless garment (vv. 23-24). The third and central scene reports Jesus' gift of Mother to Son and Son to Mother (vv. 25-27). Events leading up to Jesus' death, and his bowing his head and handing down the Spirit follow (vv. 28-30). The scene at the Cross of Jesus closes with the piercing of Jesus' side, the flow of blood and water, the fulfillment of Scripture, and the promise that they shall gaze upon the one they have pierced (vv. 31-37). Jesus' death is not so much about what happened to him, but what that event does for his followers. The episode unfolds as follows:

> *Verses* 16b-22: Jesus publicly proclaimed as king in the sign on the Cross.
> *Verses* 23-24: A garment that will not be torn apart.
> ***Verses* 25-27: Mother-Son and Son-Mother.**
> *Verses* 28-30: The death of Jesus.
> *Verses* 31-37: Consequences of the death of Jesus.

---

[1] For a more detailed presentation of the fundamental importance of the mission of Jesus for an understanding of the mission of the disciples, best summed up in 20:21: "As the Father has sent me, so I send you," see Moloney, *Love in the Gospel of John*, 37-69.

[2] For an earlier form of what follows, see Moloney, *Love in the Gospel of John*, 137-60.

Properly to interpret the central scene (19:25-27), it is necessary to glance at the previous scene (vv. 23-24), and the one that follows (vv. 28-30). There is a long tradition that regards the seamless garment that must not be torn apart in vv. 23-24 as a symbol of the Christian community, founded in vv. 25-27. It cannot be torn apart.[3] It is difficult to be certain on the text alone. The audience must proceed further into the story to discover its significance within the broader context of the Johannine passion narrative. The following interpretation of vv. 25-27 will endorse the "community" interpretation of vv. 23-24.[4] With that sign of a community that will not be torn apart (vv. 23-24) in place, we can turn to vv. 25-27. This is the last time "the hour" is mentioned in the Gospel of John (see earlier, 2:4; 7:6; 8:20; 12:23; 13:1; 17:1).

Women are at the foot of the Cross: the Mother of Jesus, her sister Mary, the wife of Clopas, and Mary Magdalene (v. 25). Only one woman remains in the action that follows, the Mother of Jesus. The "lifted up" crucified Jesus gives a significant role to two important characters from the earlier story. From his throne on the Cross (vv. 16b-22), Jesus speaks to the woman who was the first to commit herself unconditionally to the word of Jesus (see 2:3-5), and commands her, in terms that recall 2:4 ("woman") to see (Greek: *ide*) the Beloved Disciple, and to accept him as her son (v. 26). He then turns to the Beloved Disciple, by now clearly indicated for the audience the model disciple who has lain close to the breast of Jesus at the Last Supper (see 13:23). Jesus repeats his command. He is to see (Greek: *ide*) the Mother of Jesus and accept her as his Mother (v. 27a). This "formula" of

---

[3] See especially Cyprian, *De unitate Ecclesiae*, 7 (PL 4:520-21) and Augustine, *In Joannem*, 118:4 (PL 35:1949).

[4] For an exhaustive survey of the history of interpretation of vv. 23-25a, see Raymond E. Brown, *The Death of the Messiah: From Gethsemane to the Grave: A Commentary on the Passion Narratives of the Four Gospels*, 2 vols., Anchor Bible Reference Library (New York: Doubleday, 1994), 2:955-58. Brown agrees that a community interpretation is possible, given the context.

a command to "see," and act as a consequence of that seeing continues a biblical pattern of a revelatory experience.

The pattern of the command and subsequent action is part of the revelation of the design of God. Jesus' words are unquestioningly obeyed. John reports the response of the Mother of Jesus and the Beloved Disciple to Jesus' commands: "And because of (or "from") that hour the disciple took her into his own home" (v. 27b). The audience is aware that the Cross is "the hour of Jesus" (see 2:4; 7:6, 30; 8:20; 12:23; 13:1; 17:1). Given the tension generated in the narrative by the steady *forward-looking* use of "the hour" from an event that was "not yet" (2:4; 7:6, 30; 8:20) to its arrival (12:23; 13:1; 16:21; 17:1; 19:30), it is not likely that the use of the expression "the hour" in this intense moment in the Johannine passion story simply means a point of time after which the Beloved Disciple looks after the Mother of Jesus. The audience has been told too often that "the hour has come" (12:23; 13:1; 16:21; 17:1) to read v. 27 in this trivial way. Something more than a domestic arrangement is established at "the hour" of the Cross.

Returning to the Greek, v. 27b: "and because (from) that hour" (*ap'ekeinēs tēs hōras*), is open to two translations. One of these interpretations is almost universally accepted by the translators and commentators; the other is rarely present in discussions of this passage. There is no doubt that the expression has a temporal meaning: "from that particular time." But the other possible translation catches the theological and dramatic significance of "the hour of Jesus." It depends upon the interpretation of the Greek preposition *apo*, followed by the genitive case (as here) as causal: "because of that hour."[5] The remaining words of v. 27 suggest that "the hour" in this context must be the "cause" of something. *As a result of* the lifting up

---

5 For this causal meaning of "because of" for *apo* with the genitive, see Blass, Debrunner, and Funk, *A Greek Grammar of the New Testament*, 113, § 210.

of Jesus on the Cross, the Beloved Disciple and the Mother of Jesus are united as the Beloved Disciple takes the Mother of Jesus "to his own home (*eis ta idia*)." The audience recalls the situation described in the Prologue, where the Word came "to his own home" (*eis ta idia*) but was not received (1:11). Now, as the story of Jesus draws to an end, that situation has been reversed. *Because of* "the hour" of Jesus' being lifted up and exalted (see 3:14; 8:28; 12:32) he now has a "home."

At the Cross a new family of Jesus has been created. The Mother of Jesus, a model of faith, and the disciple whom Jesus loved and held close to himself, are united as the Mother accepts the disciple and the disciple accepts the Mother. At the Cross and because of the Cross the lifted up Son of Man established a new family. Among the many commentators on the Fourth Gospel, Sir Edwyn Hoskyns has eloquently expressed the meaning of vv. 25-27:

> At the time of the Lord's death a new family is brought into being. If the unity of the Church is symbolised by the seamless robe, the peculiar nature of that unity is indicated here. The Church proceeds from the sacrifice of the Son of God, and the union of the Beloved Disciple and the Mother of the Lord prefigures and foreshadows the charity of the *Ecclesia* of God.[6]

At this supreme moment of a revelation of love (see 3:16; 13:1; 15:13), a community of love is founded *because of the hour*.

Gathering at the Cross

A theme of "gathering," has developed over the final episodes of Jesus' public ministry. During the discourse on the Good Shepherd, Jesus

---

6   Edwyn C. Hoskyns, *The Fourth Gospel*, ed. Francis N. Davey (London: Faber & Faber, 1947), 530.

announced that his death would bring other sheep, not of the fold of Israel, to form one flock, with one shepherd (10:14-16). After Caiaphas' prophetic words that Jesus would die for the nation, John enlarges that vision: he was to die "not for the nation only, but to gather into one the dispersed children of God" (11:52). As Greeks ask to see him, Jesus announces that the hour has come, and that the grain of wheat that dies will produce much fruit (12:20-24). His being lifted up will draw everyone to himself (12:32-33). This theme is resumed and brought to conclusion in the passion narrative.

Jesus' crucifixion is described as a gathering. The event of the physical crucifixion is very sparsely narrated, in three Greek words (*hopou auton estaurōsen*: "there they crucified him"). But this terseness throws into relief the lengthy and complicated description of the fact that he is crucified between two others. John goes to considerable lengths, even to the point of grammatical clumsiness, to indicate Jesus' role at the center of the scene. A literal translation of the Greek produces: "and with him two others, one on either side, and Jesus between them (*kai met'autou allous duo enteuthen kai enteuthen, meson de ton Iēsoun*)" (19:18). The gathering has begun. "In his very 'lifting up' there is a gathering, and he is at its centre."[7] The theme of the future gathering of a community returns as a major theme across the passion narrative. Its future unity is indicated in the episode of the seamless garment (19:23-25), its future nourishment in the blood and the water flowing from the side of the pierced Jesus. Because of the event of the Cross, they will gaze upon the one they have pierced (v. 37). Enthroned on the Cross, the gift of Mother to disciple and disciple to Mother at the Cross (19:25-27) brings the gathering, with significant ecclesial allusions, to its conclusion. Only now, when the gathering promised by Jesus during

---

7   Francis J. Moloney, *The Gospel of John*, Sacra Pagina 4 (Collegeville: Liturgical Press, 1998), 502.

his public ministry has been established in the union of the first of all believers (the Mother of Jesus) and the disciple whom Jesus loved, can Jesus call out in death, "It is finished" (19:30a). Jesus has brought to perfection the task given him by the Father (see 4:34). The hour has come and a new family of God has begun at the foot of the Cross. It is upon this family that he pours down the Spirit (v. 30b) and gifts them with the blood and water which flow from his side (vv. 34-35). The community emerges from the darkness as Joseph of Arimathea and Nicodemus, no longer "secret disciples" courageously accost Roman authority, ask for the body and bury the deceased Jesus as a king, in a new tomb where no one had been laid (vv. 38-41).

It Is Finished!

In 19:28-30 the audience is bombarded with the steady repetition of two verbs that mean "to bring to an end, to perfect, to fulfill, to consummate," both of which are related to the noun *telos* (see 4:34; 5:36; 13:1; 17:4). In 19:28 Jesus knows that everything is now finished (*tetelestai*). In order to bring scripture to fulfillment (*teleiōthēi*), he received the vinegar (v. 29), and then said: "It is finished" (*tetelestai*) (v. 30). Jesus' words that mark the "end" of his life recall the words of the narrator from 13:1: "When Jesus knew that his hour had come to depart out of this world to the Father, having loved his own who were in the world, he loved them *to the end* (*eis telos*)." Jesus' final cry, "It is finished" (v. 30) is an exclamation of achievement, almost of triumph. The task given to him by his Father (see 4:34; 5:36; 17:4), has now been consummately brought to its conclusion. In this moment of death "he bowed his head and handed down the Spirit (*paredōken to pneuma*)" (v. 30).

At the Feast of Tabernacles, as Jesus promised living water, the Spirit had not yet been given because Jesus had not yet been glorified (7:39). In the glorification of God that takes place in the lifting up of the

Son of Man (see 13:31-32), the Spirit is given (19:30). The translation "gave up his spirit" is universally present in modern translations of 19:30. Influenced by Mark, Matthew, and Luke, translators read the expression as a way of describing Jesus' death. This is certainly the case with Mark's "he breathed his last" (Mark 15:37: *exepneusen*), an expression repeated by Luke 23:46. Matthew has the more elegant "he yielded up the spirit" (Matt 27:50: *aphēken to pneuma*). In all three Synoptic Gospels the "spirit" named is the human life of Jesus that comes to an end. This is not the case in John 19:30, as the Greek verb used has a primary meaning of "hand over, to give (over), deliver, entrust."[8] Equally important, the Greek text does not say "his spirit" (*to pneuma autou*), but "the Spirit" (*to pneuma*). In handing down "the Spirit" Jesus brings to perfection the task which the Father had given to him. Jesus hands over, entrusts, *the* Spirit to his new family (v. 30), gathered at the foot of the Cross (see vv. 25-27).

The final scene at the Cross has two major elements. In a first moment, the day of Preparation for the Passover necessitates that the Romans remove the crucified from their place of torture (v. 31). The two who had been crucified with Jesus have their legs broken, but this does not happen to Jesus. As he is already dead, his side is pierced with a lance, and blood and water flow from his pierced side (vv. 31-34). Secondly, Scripture is fulfilled, as the Passover Lamb is slain without a bone being broken (see Ps 34:20-21; Exod 12:10, 46; Num 9:12). Once allowance is made for the fulfillment of the Scriptures concerning the Passover Lamb, this simple narrative could be no more than a reporting of facts, as everything could have taken place as described, including the blood and the water flowing from the side of Jesus.[9]

---

8   See Danker, *Greek-English Lexicon*, 761-63, s.v. *paradidōmi*.
9   For physical explanations of the blood and water, see John Wilkinson, "The Incident of the Blood and Water in John 19.34," *Scottish Journal of Theology* 28 (1975): 149-72.

But the narrator unexpectedly launches into a personal comment which has no parallel in the rest of the Gospel story. The Beloved Disciple insists on his witness, and on the truthfulness of his testimony. It is important to him that his audience accept what they have been told – "that you also may believe" (v. 35). The blood and the water must mean something to the audience, and the narrator is anxious that there be no doubt about the blood and the water that flowed from the crucified Jesus. Jesus has entrusted the Spirit to the community; now he entrusts the blood and the water of Eucharist and baptism. The author presupposes the audience's knowledge and experience of the "water" of baptism (see 3:5; 13:1-11) and the "blood" of Eucharist (see 6:53, 54, 55-56), and links them with the Cross. The Johannine passion account deals both with what happened to Jesus, and how this founded a community of the followers of Jesus. The physical *absence* of the historical Jesus to the community at the end of the first century lies behind the narrator's passionate intervention in v. 35. Despite Jesus' *physical* absence, he is present in the blood and the water of their community practices. They were given to them in and through the death of Jesus. In its celebration of baptism and Eucharist the community finds the presence of the absent one and thus gaze upon the one whom they have pierced (v. 37. See Zech 12:10).

The urgency of this question for a community which no longer sees Jesus has led to the intervention of the narrator in v. 35. He looks back to the founding event of the Christian community: "He who saw it has borne witness – his testimony is true, and he knows that he tells the truth - *that you also may believe.*" John is speaking to the Church of all ages, founded at the Cross. Through the witness of the Beloved Disciple, we have access to the founding event of the Christian community that took place at the Cross.

THE FOUNDATION OF THE CHURCH'S MISSION: JOHN 20:19-23

The formal beginnings of the Church's mission take place as the risen Jesus speaks to his disciples in 20:19-23.[10] Prepared by Mary Magdalene's Easter message (v. 18), the crucified and risen Jesus appears among them (vv. 19-20). They receive his peace, and Jesus tells them that as the Father had sent Jesus, he now sends them (vv. 19-21. See also 13:18-20; 17:18-19). Given the importance of Jesus' promise in the last discourse of 14:1–16:33 to give the disciples his "peace" (see 14:27 [twice]; 16:33), the greeting of Jesus in 20:19, 21, 26 must be seen as a fulfillment of that promise, also taking place as the "hour" concludes. The same process of fulfillment is also indicated by the joy of the disciples "when they saw the Lord" (v. 22). Throughout his discourse he has told them of the joy that would flow from his departure from them (15:11; 16:20, 21, 22 [verb "rejoice" and noun "joy"], 24; 17:13). However fragile, full of the peace and joy generated by the "hour," they are his sent ones, the bearers of his word (see 18:21), and whoever receives them will receive both Jesus and the one who sent him (see 13:20).

The gift of the Spirit defines the foundation of the Church's mission. The command that they continue his critical presence in the world as they forgive and retain sin accompanies this further gift of the Spirit (vv. 22-23). Jesus' breathing upon them recalls the moment of creation in LXX Genesis 2:7 (see also LXX Ezek 37:9-10; Wis 15:11). They receive his peace that produces joy (vv. 19-20), they are commissioned as sent ones of Jesus, just as he was the sent one of the Father (v. 21), and they receive the Spirit. They are to repeat Jesus' judging presence in the world during his absence (vv. 22-23).

As we have seen, Jesus bestows the Spirit upon the symbolic infant Church, the Mother and the Disciple, a new family at the foot of the

---

10 See, for more detail, Moloney, *Love in the Gospel of John*, 167-70.

Cross (19:30). Not all interpreters accept that the Spirit is given at the Cross as it is given in 20:22. They claim that Jesus cannot give the Spirit twice. Recognition of the fact that both 19:30 and 20:22 form part of Jesus' "hour" makes the question of "two gifts of the Spirit" irrelevant. The gift of the Spirit, promised across the Gospel, and especially in the Paraclete sayings in the discourse of 14:1–16:33, cannot be limited to 20:22 which is closely tied to the authority of the disciples to forgive and retain sin (v. 23). The Spirit Paraclete offers more to the disciples of Jesus than their role as the ongoing presence of Jesus' light (see 9:4).[11] The Spirit is "another Paraclete." It ensures the revealing presence of Jesus (14:16-17), teaching all things, calling to their remembrance what Jesus has said (14:26), witnessing Jesus' presence to them as they witness (15:26-27). The Spirit guides into all truth and glorifies the absent Jesus by taking what was of Jesus and passing it on to the disciples (16:13-14). "The community and all its members is Jesus at work in the world and his work is to take away sins by giving life in all its fullness."[12] At the Cross, the Spirit is poured down upon the community of faith and love in a *foundational*

---

11 This sentence succinctly suggests my interpretation of v. 23. The meaning of "If you forgive the sins of any, they are forgiven; if you retain the sins of any, they are retained" is a problem for Johannine interpreters. It has been further complicated by the Roman Catholic identification of this passage as a biblical basis for the sacrament of reconciliation. The interpretation suggested above is that after Jesus returns to the Father, his critical presence in the world, bringing light into darkness that is sometimes accepted and sometimes rejected, will continue in the experience of the disciples. Put positively, they will continue to be the *critical presence* of the revelation of God in their mission, thus forgiving and retaining (see 15:18–16:3). Raymond E. Brown, *The Gospel According to John*, 2 vols., Anchor Bible 29-29A (Garden City, NY: Doubleday, 1966-1970), 2:1044 puts it well: "The power to isolate, repel and negate evil and sin, a power given to Jesus by the Father, and given in turn by Jesus through the gift of the spirit to those whom he commissions." The critical exposure of right and wrong that results from the gift of the Paraclete is developed at greater length in 16:7-11. See Moloney, *John*, 440-41, 445-47. An interesting alternative view has been proposed by Sandra M. Schneiders, *Jesus Risen in Our Midst. Essays on the Resurrection in the Fourth Gospel* (Collegeville: Liturgical Press, 2013), 113-15. Accepting the primary meaning of the Greek verb *krateō* as "to hold fast," she suggests that it has little to do with "retaining" (an interpretation influenced by Matt 18:18). She suggests the translation/interpretation "those [the forgiven] whom you hold fast [in the communion of the Church] are held fast" (p. 114). See also pp. 133-41.

12 Sandra M. Schneiders, "The Resurrection (of the Body) in the Fourth Gospel: A Key to Johannine Spirituality," in *Life in Abundance: Studies in John's Gospel in Tribute to Raymond E. Brown*, ed. John R. Donahue (Collegeville: Liturgical Press, 2005), 187.

moment of the Church, set within the context of the "hour." As risen Lord, equally part of the "hour," Jesus establishes and initiates *the mission* to continue his critical presence in the world during the time of his absence. Jesus' promise of the Paraclete requires both foundation moments.

> The oneness of the hour and all that is achieved by and through it is nowhere clearer to the reader than in these two episodes that take place at the hour: the founding gift of the Spirit (19:30; see 14:16-17) and the commissioning of the disciples who have been with him from the beginning to be his witnesses empowered by the Spirit. (20:22; see 15:26-27)[13]

Jesus has made visible the love of God on the Cross, and by means of the Cross and resurrection he will be glorified by returning to the Father and the glory which was his before the foundation of the world (11:4; 12:23, 27-28; 13:1; 17:1-5). He has founded a Spirit-filled community of disciples and has commissioned them to continue his mission (19:30; 20:22-23).

AUTHORITY IN THE JOHANNINE CHURCH – JOHN 21:15-24

The story of Jesus told in 1:1–20:31 left some crucial issues unresolved, especially concerning the nature of the ongoing life of the community of faith and love founded at the Cross (19:25-27), commissioned to continue the presence of the light in the world (20:19-23. See 9:4). Across the Gospel Jesus has issued only two commandments: believe and love (see 13:34; 14:1, 11, 15, 21; 15:10, 12; 16:27, 31). They are

---

[13] Francis J. Moloney, *Glory Not Dishonor. Reading John 13-21* (Minneapolis: Fortress, 1998), 172.

both essential to Christianity, but a community needs more than belief and love to exist – both in itself, and in its relationships with the world around it. Some leadership, and subsequent discipline is called for. Later in the life of that community tensions must have emerged around the respective roles of the Beloved Disciple and Peter. John 21 must be regarded as a necessary epilogue to John 1–20. Half of it is dedicated to the questions of their role and their authority.[14]

Simon Peter: The Shepherd

Jesus' thrice-repeated question asks Simon Peter to commit himself to love Jesus more than he loves anything else. Peter responds unconditionally, confessing that his love for Jesus is known by the all-knowing risen Lord. Jesus commands Peter to pasture his sheep. A relationship between the role of Peter and the role of Jesus the Good Shepherd of 10:1-18 is established. Jesus repeats this same question, answer, and imperative three times (vv. 15-17). The major reason for Jesus' demanding a threefold confession of love is Peter's threefold denial of Jesus at the outset of the passion narrative (cf. 18:15-18, 25-27). However fragile, Peter has been close to Jesus throughout the ministry (cf. 1:40-42; 6:67-69; 13:6-10, 36-38; 18:15), a closeness dramatically destroyed by the disciple's threefold denial and the subsequent events of the crucifixion of Jesus (18:15-19, 25-27). The royal lifting up of Jesus on the Cross, the foundation of a new family of God and the gift of the Spirit (19:17-37), have been marked by the presence of the Beloved Disciple (cf. 19:25-27) – and the absence of Simon Peter! The rhythmic threefold repetition of the same question contains the hint of an accusation: "you once denied me ... are you sure of your relationship to me now?"

---

14 See Moloney, *Love in the Gospel of John*, 181-87. See also Francis J. Moloney, "'For as yet They Did Not Know the Scripture' (John 20:9): A Study in Narrative Time," *The Irish Theological Quarterly* 79 (2014): 97-111.

Essential to that relationship is love for Jesus (see 8:42; 14:21, 23-24 [framed positively and negatively], 28; 16:27). In the dynamism of love within the Fourth Gospel, the disciple must love the Son, as the Son loves the Father and the Father loves the Son. Only when that dynamism of love is in place is Jesus' request of the Father in 17:24-26 possible. There Jesus prayed that the Father might sweep the disciples into the love that exists between the Father and the Son. A relationship of love must be established between Peter and Jesus. Peter's heartfelt protestations of love leads to the establishment of a that relationship: Jesus appoints Peter as the one who shepherds his sheep. As Rekha Chennattu remarks: "The threefold profession of love and commitment on the part of Peter therefore reinforces the idea that Peter's unconditional love for Jesus is the foundation and source of his mission as the shepherd of the new covenant community."[15]

Peter is to be "shepherd," "feeding" the "lambs" and "sheep" of Jesus. This mission of leadership will cost him no less than everything (vv. 18-19). Introduced by the Johannine double "amen," Jesus reminds Peter of a time in the past, during the ministry of Jesus, when Peter showed a great deal of good will (especially 6:67-69), but ultimately went into denial. There is a danger that such a situation might repeat itself. After all that has been told in 1:1–20:31, at the beginning of chapter 21 Peter announces, "I am going fishing," and a group of disciples reply, "We will go with you" (21:3). Has everything been forgotten? There was a time when Peter was young, when he girded himself and went where he would (v. 18a). He has now overcome the scandal of his rejection of Jesus and has unconditionally committed himself to the way of the Good Shepherd (vv. 15-17). The time will come, "when you are old," when Peter will lay down his life for the sheep of Jesus entrusted to his care. Another will gird him and carry him where he would prefer

---

[15] Rekha M. Chennattu, *Johannine Discipleship as a Covenant Relationship* (Peabody, MA: Hendrickson, 2006), 178.

not to go. By the time of the writing of this episode Peter had already stretched out his hands. An executioner had girded him with a cross, and he had laid down his life for the flock of Jesus.

Simon Peter's commitment to the way of the Good Shepherd associates him with the death of Jesus. Death did not fall upon Jesus as a terrible end to a self-sacrificed life. His unconditional acceptance of the will of the Father (cf. 4:34; 5:36; 17:4) revealed the love of God for the world (3:16). God was glorified (cf. 11:4, 40; 12:28; 13:31-32; 17:1-5) as Jesus gave his life (cf. 11:4; 12:23; 13:31-32; 17:1-5). Peter's unconditional acceptance of the role as shepherd of the sheep of Jesus (vv. 15-17) will also lead to the glorification of God in his self-gift in love unto death (v. 19a). The link between Peter and Jesus reaches beyond the pasturing task of the Good Shepherd; Peter is also to glorify God by his death, as Jesus did by his death (v. 19a. See 11:4; 12:27-28; 13:31-32). There is little else for Jesus to do but invite Peter to follow him down this way (v. 19b). This "following" has a physical meaning, as Peter walks behind Jesus (cf. v. 20a), but it also means an "undeviating discipleship all the rest of his days,"[16] that follows Jesus' revelation of the love of God by loving his sheep as Jesus has loved him (13:34-35; 15:12, 17).

The Beloved Disciple: The Witness

Responding to the call to "follow" Jesus in v. 20, Peter does what Jesus had commanded in v. 19. However, as he follows he turns and sees the Beloved Disciple, described as the one who had lain close to Jesus' breast and had been asked for the identity of the betrayer (see 13:23-25). He is also "following" (v. 20). These two figures, one whose love for Jesus has just been re-established (vv. 15-17), and the other whose love

---

[16] George R. Beasley-Murray, *John*, Word Biblical Commentary 36 (Waco, TX: Word Books, 1987), 409.

has never been in question (13:23-25; 19:25-27; 20:2-9), are paired as "followers" of Jesus. Peter poses a question that Jesus will answer in v. 22. His response is clarified by the narrator in vv. 23-24: "Lord, what about this man?" (v. 21). The question of the relative roles of these two disciples emerges. A post-Easter Johannine community of "followers," aware that they have all been commanded to love as Jesus has loved, looks back upon these two foundational figures, and asks about the relative significance of their leadership roles in the ongoing life of love which lies at the heart of their vocation (see 13:34-35; 15:12-17).

Peter's confession of love for Jesus firmly established a disciple and a pastor (vv. 15-17). Questions remain around his relationship with the figure of the Beloved Disciple. The paths of these two characters have been entwined across the latter part of the Gospel, at the last meal (13:23-25), in the court of the high priest (18:15-16), and at the empty tomb (cf. 20:3-10). On those earlier occasions, despite Peter's obvious importance, the Beloved Disciple held pride of place (13:23; 18:15-16; 20:4, 8). As the role of the Beloved Disciple at the final meal, the Cross, and at the empty tomb indicates, the community whose Jesus-story is found in the Gospel of John regarded the Beloved Disciple as a founding figure of the community (cf. 19:25-27).[17] However, if the story has reported that Peter was appointed disciple and pastor of the community as a result of his love for Jesus (vv. 15-17), not only Peter *in the story* but also the audience receiving this Gospel in the life of the Church over the centuries might ask: "What about this man?" (v. 21).

The community has in its recorded memory of Jesus' words a promise that the Beloved Disciple would not die before Jesus' return. It needs correction. The exact words of Jesus are: "If it is my will that he remain until I come, what is that to you? Follow me!" (v. 22). Jesus

---

[17] On the Beloved Disciple, see R. Alan Culpepper, *John, the Son of Zebedee. The Life of a Legend*, Studies on Personalities of the New Testament (Columbia, SC: University of South Carolina Press, 1994).

challenges Peter to maintain his role as a follower of Jesus, not to worry about the destiny of the Beloved Disciple. Jesus' words to him in vv. 18-19 indicate his destiny. Central to Jesus' words, comments the narrator, is the conditional: *"If it is my will."* Jesus did not say that the Beloved Disciple would not die before the coming of Jesus. Jesus' will determines his future. The problem behind this clarification of what Jesus had said is the death of the Beloved Disciple. "The saying spread abroad ... that this disciple was not to die" (v. 23a). This "saying," this expression of popular opinion, was based on a faulty understanding of Jesus' earlier words. The Beloved Disciple is no longer alive, and the community should not wonder at his death. Whatever has happened to the Beloved Disciple was the fulfillment of the will of Jesus for him. Both Peter (cf. vv. 18-19) and the Beloved Disciple (vv. 22-23) have died, but they have *both* been established by Jesus as foundational figures of a future community of disciples commanded to love as Jesus loved (13:34-35; 15:12, 17) – because of their love for Jesus (21:7, 15-17, 20).

The narrator has more to say about the Beloved Disciple. Matching Jesus' establishment of Peter as pastor and disciple whose love for Jesus will lead him to death (vv. 15-19), the final words from the narrator clarify the significance of the Beloved Disciple. The Beloved Disciple is the author of the community's story of the life and teaching, death and resurrection of Jesus (v. 24). Living in the in-between-time, after the death and departure of Jesus, and the deaths of Peter and the Beloved Disciple, the community has a link between the events of the past and the experience of the present provided by the Beloved Disciple's witness. He was a disciple of Jesus who both witnessed "these things," and then transmitted "these things." The witnessing of what was written is still present because of the past action of the

Beloved Disciple.[18] The community can be confident of the truth of their Jesus-story.

Peter is the appointed shepherd of the flock, called to love to the point of death (cf. vv. 15-19), while the Beloved Disciple is the bearer of the authentic Jesus tradition (v. 24). Both are crucial to a community of disciples called to love as Jesus loved (13:15, 34-35; 15:12, 17). However, their ministries are different. The ministry of the Beloved Disciple has been to witness to Jesus in a way that goes on generating life and love. The ministry of Peter is to shepherd the flock. The former is a charismatic role, the latter the equally difficult task of governing and caring.

MISSION

For John, the "lifting up" of the Son of Man on the Cross is the supreme revelation of God's love, manifested in Jesus' love for his own "to the end" at the "hour" (13:1 [*eis telos*]. See 17:1, 4 [*teleiōsas*]). From his throne on the Cross he creates a new family, a new home among men and women, founded upon the woman who believed and the disciple he loved (19:25-27). His steady promise that he would gather others, indeed draw all humankind to himself on the Cross (10:16; 11:52; 12:24, 32-33), is fulfilled in the "gathering" of the crucifixion (19:18), and the formation of his new family at the Cross (19:25-27). He pours down the Spirit upon the members of the new family (19:30), and gives them the waters of baptism and the blood of Eucharist so that they might believe, and gaze upon the one they have pierced (19:31-37). Across that single "hour" of death and resurrection he both *founds* the Church (19:25-27), and *commissions* it in the upper

---

[18] On the Beloved Disciple as the "writer" of the text as we have it today, see Moloney, *John*, 561-62, and the discussion documented there.

room, sending his disciples, as he has been sent (20:22-23). They will do what he has done: make God known in the world, under the direction of a shepherd who professes his love, and a witness who is loved (21:15-24).

Jesus' self-gift in love generates the gift of the *founding* and *missioning* Spirit in the Church. Love is also the source of the charismatic presence of the Beloved Disciple and the governing presence of Peter. The Beloved Disciple's witness to the experience of love, and the loving unto death of Simon Peter, are the bedrock upon which all subsequent mission is to be constructed. Disciples of Jesus are to follow the example that he has given them (13:15), responding to his commandment: "A new commandment I give to you, that you love one another; even as I have loved you, that you also love one another. By this everyone will know that you are my disciples, if you have love for one another" (13:34-35. See also 15:12, 17).

6

THE CELEBRATION OF THE EUCHARIST AT THE HEART OF THE CHRISTIAN MISSION

"As often as you shall eat this bread and drink this cup, you proclaim the Lord's death until he comes"
(1 Cor 11:26)

Christian communities celebrated the Lord's Supper from their earliest days. The situation Paul addresses in Corinth, while not very flattering, is our earliest written testimony to the practice of celebrating the Eucharist. Paul wrote this first of his letters to the Christians in Corinth in the early 50s of the first century. Even though this was only 20 years after the death of Jesus, Paul already regards what he is passing on to the Corinthians as part of what can be called *Jesus tradition*. He tells them: "For I received from the Lord what I also delivered to you, that the Lord Jesus on the night he was betrayed took bread …" (1 Cor 11:23). Unlike the Gospels, where the report of Jesus' final meal with his disciples is set within a broader narrative of his life, death and resurrection, Paul's only reference to Jesus' words on that night is: "This is my body broken for you. Do this in remembrance of me" (1 Cor 11:24), and "This cup is the new covenant in my blood. Do this, as often as you drink it, in remembrance of me" (11:25).

The three Synoptic Gospels report a final meal, shared by Jesus and the disciples, during which Jesus takes elements from a traditional ritual meal (and possibly a Passover Meal), bread and wine (Mark 14:17-31; Matt 26:20-35; Luke 22:14-38). Instead of looking to the past to explain the significance of the elements (the bread as a memory of the manna in the desert and the wine as a memory of the opening of the Reed Sea), Jesus points forward to his death: the bread is his broken body and the wine is his spilled blood "for" others. All the records of this meal indicate, by means of the preposition "for/for the sake of" (Greek: *hyper*), that this death is in some way "for others." This is not only the case for the three Synoptic Gospels (Mark 14:24; Matt 26:28; Luke 22:19), but it is also found in words that probably reflect the Johannine Eucharistic tradition (John 6:51c: "the bread that I will give is my flesh for the life of the world" AT), and certainly in the tradition found in Paul (see 1 Cor 11:24). There are accounts of such meals celebrated in the Jerusalem Church in the Acts of the Apostles (see Acts 2:42-47; 20:7-11; 27:33-36). Luke wrote these reports in the late 80s of the first century. He looks back upon a well-established practice within the Christian tradition and tells of the meals celebrated in Jerusalem as an idealized portrait of love and unity that existed in the founding Christian community. These accounts call Christians of all ages to pursue these ideals.

As well as these explicit "meal contexts," during which Jesus shares bread and wine with his disciples, there are other scenes in the Gospel traditions that reflect a Eucharistic background. The multiplication of the loaves and fishes in the Synoptics (Mark 6:31-44; 8:1-9; Matt

14:13-21; 15:32-39; Luke 9:10-17), and the Johannine Passover multiplication of the loaves and fishes (John 6:1-15 [for the Passover, see v. 4]), as well as Jesus' gift of the morsel to the disciples, including Judas, in John 13:21-30 reflect the early Church's easy use of language and symbolism that came from a practice central to their emerging uniqueness: the celebration of the Eucharistic meal "for others." The evidence for the origins of this early Christian cultic practice in the life of Jesus is overwhelming. The various forms of Christianity, reflected in the different traditions found in Paul, Mark, Matthew, Luke, and John took it for granted that Jesus founded a meal tradition that we know as the celebration of the Lord's Supper "for others" – the Eucharist, or the more missionary expression "the Mass," from the Latin verb "to send" (*mittere*).

There is no evidence for a specifically Christian priesthood in the New Testament.[1] Jesus Christ gave us a meal that we celebrate in his memory. He called all believers to celebrate and live Eucharist. All Christians must recognize that they are a Eucharistic people. An ordained ministry emerged later in the history of the Church as ministers in a community. But prior to that development, Christians understood themselves as loved by God, freed from their sins by the blood of Jesus Christ, "a kingdom of priests serving his God and Father" (Rev. 1:5-6; 5:10).

OUR EUCHARISTIC ORIGINS

From the very beginnings of Christianity, the baptized were called to a priesthood associated with the self-gift of the believer "for others," in imitation of Jesus Christ who freed us from our sins through his

---

1 For a brief study of the development of an ordained priesthood, focused upon the celebration of the Eucharist, see Francis J. Moloney, *Broken for You. Jesus Christ, the Catholic Priesthood and the Word of God* (Bayswater, VIC: Coventry Press, 2018), 29-52.

loving response to his Father. As he was our Priest (see Heb 5:6-10; 7:1-28; 8:4-6; 10:11-22), so are those who commit themselves to follow him made priests, serving our God and Father, freed from sins by the blood of Jesus (see Rev 1:5-6; 5:10). Our common priesthood is intimately associated with our being a Eucharistic people. An overview of the New Testament witness to our Eucharistic origins makes this clear. It also locates the celebration of the Eucharist at the heart of all Christian mission.

Saint Paul

Throughout 1 Corinthians Paul addresses problems which have arisen in the community at Corinth.[2] In Paul's discussion of the Corinthians' problematic celebration of the Lord's supper he first attacks the nature of their abuse of the Eucharistic table in 11:17-22. He then reports his tradition of the Eucharistic words (vv. 23-26). More theological conclusions and recommendations close his treatment (vv. 27-34). In vv. 27-28 Paul warns against eating the bread and drinking the cup of the Lord in an "unworthy manner," drawing conclusions from the abuses he described in vv. 17-22. "I hear that there are divisions among you" (v. 18). These divisions are described as follows: "In eating, each one goes ahead with his own meal, and one is hungry and another is drunk. What! Do you not have houses to eat and drink in? Or do you despise the Church of God and humiliate those who have nothing? What shall I say to you? Shall I commend you in this? No I shall not!" (vv. 21-22). The Lord's supper was supposed to be a common meal, but Paul has heard that this has become impossible at Corinth because divisions between the wealthy and the poor existed to such an extent that no one was concerned about the other. It would be better for the Corinthians to eat in their own houses, rather than

---

[2] For a more extensive treatment of what follows, see Moloney, *Body Broken for a Broken People*, 41-69.

pretend a unity in their Eucharistic celebration which their behavior belies. In addition to humiliating "those who have nothing," they show they hold true community in contempt. This is the "unworthy manner" of participating in the Eucharist chastised by Paul in v. 27, and the reason for the request that a person should "examine himself" expressed in v. 28.

Within this context of instruction and warning, Paul inserts his tradition of the Eucharistic words of Jesus (vv. 23-26). They are highlighted by the command, repeated over both the bread and the wine, to perform the action of breaking the bread and sharing the cup "in remembrance of me" (vv. 24 and 25). The twice repeated command is a challenge to an appreciation of the Eucharistic nature of the Christian life. To celebrate Eucharist is to commit oneself to a discipleship which "remembers" Jesus – not only in the breaking of the ritual bread and sharing the ritual cup – but also in "imitation" of Jesus, in the ongoing breaking of one's own body and spilling of one's own blood "in remembrance" of Jesus. For this reason, Paul adds: "You proclaim the Lord's death until he comes" (v. 26). In the broken body and the spilled blood of a Church of disciples who live the Eucharist the Lord's death is proclaimed in the world, until he comes again.

Paul's call for unity in 1 Corinthians 11:17-22 is a summons motivated by the need for the Corinthian community "to remember," to practice at the level of life what they proclaim at the level of ritual (vv. 23-26). To continue in their present practice would be to eat the bread and drink the cup "unworthily" (v. 27). Thus they must examine themselves carefully on these issues before approaching the Eucharistic meal (v. 28).

In v. 29 Paul warns the Corinthians: "Anyone who eats and drinks without discerning the body eats and drinks judgment upon himself." Not to discern the body is to fail to recognize the Lord's presence in the Eucharist in the sense of the Lord who died for us (see v. 24: "This is my body which is for [*hyper*] you"). But "body" also means the community. Ignoring the "body" of Christ, present in the "body" of the community in their Eucharistic meals, the Corinthians proclaim the presence of the Lord in a lie that offends against the "rhythm" of the offering of Christ which they claim to be "remembering" in their celebration. Christians are called to repeat the self-gift of Christ in his memory both in cult and in life. Not to celebrate Eucharist in this way is to "eat and drink judgment" upon oneself (v. 29). Not recognizing the sacrificed "body" of Jesus in the Eucharist, they offend against the "body' which is the Church, called to repeat that sacrifice in its own life.

From the very first witness we have of the celebration of the Eucharist in the community, Paul uses words from Jesus to instruct Christians that they are to look beyond themselves, to break their bodies and spill their blood "for others." Eucharist is not a private or community "cultic act." It is a call to mission, an uncompromising acceptance of God's call that we give ourselves "for others."

The Synoptic Gospels

The Gospels, written decades after Paul's First Letter to the Corinthians (Mark: c. 70; Matthew and Luke: c. 85; John: c. 100), continue to develop a rich understanding of Jesus' self-gift in love in narratives that presuppose the celebration of the Eucharist and summon those who celebrate Eucharist to follow him in his self-gift for others.

(a) The Gospels of Mark and Matthew

Mark 14:17-31, the account of the Last Supper in this Gospel, is an example of the practice of framing episodes (a "sandwich construction") that we have encountered in our chapter on Mark's presentation of the disciples in Mark 6:6b-30.³ Jesus shares a meal with his disciples (14:22-25), but the episodes before and after the meal tell of his disciples' betrayal, denial and flight (vv. 17-21; 26-31). In vv. 17-21 Jesus "came with the twelve," a group appointed in 3:14 "to be with him" (v. 17). The setting for Jesus' prediction of his betrayal is the meal table, a sacred place among friends. Jesus explains that the betrayer will be "one who is eating with me" (v. 18). Intimacy is heightened by the words of Jesus: "It is one of the twelve, one who is dipping bread in the same dish with me." A similar attention to the closeness that exists between Jesus and his future betrayers is found in vv. 26-31. He predicts they "will all fall away" (v. 27). He uses the image of the shepherd and his sheep (v. 27), and his predictions lead to expressions of love and devotion. Peter swears an unfailing loyalty, better than all the others who may fall away (v. 29). He even claims that he is prepared to lay down his life for his master (v. 31). Peter is not alone in swearing loyalty and love: "And they all said the same."

In the center of the passage, 14:22-26 reports Jesus' last meal with the disciples, who will betray, deny and abandon him (14:22-26). The theme of table fellowship with the betrayers opens the passage: "And as *they* were eating, he took bread, and blessed, and broke it, and *gave it to them.*" (v 22). This theme is continued in the sharing of the cup, where the same recipients are again specified: "And he took the cup, and when he had given thanks *he gave it to them, and they all drank of it*" (v. 23). The words over the bread and the cup point to the Cross: a body broken and blood poured out (vv. 22 and 24), but they also point to something beyond the day of crucifixion. The blood is to be a covenant (v. 24), and he comments that he will not "drink again of the fruit of the vine until that day when I drink it new in the kingdom of God" (v. 25). The word "until" rings out a message of trust

---

3   For a more extensive treatment of what follows, see Moloney, *Body Broken*, 82-97. On the framing of narratives, the so-called "sandwich constructions," see above, pp. 37-38.

and hope that looks well beyond the events of Good Friday. There is to be a body given and blood poured out which will set up a new covenant reaching beyond the Cross into the definitive establishment of the Kingdom. A covenant with whom? The body broken and the blood poured out sets up a new covenant with *the fragile disciples* who were the first recipients of that bread and cup. Mark has given us an account of Jesus' gift of himself unto death to set up a new and lasting kingdom with the characters in the story. Jesus loves his failing disciples with a love which is in no way matched by the love which they bear him.

The Gospel of Matthew repeats Mark's account of the Last Supper, almost verbatim. Matthew retains the sandwich construction, placing the sharing of the bread and wine (Matt 26:26-30) between Jesus' prophecies of the future betrayal of Judas (vv. 20-25), the denials of Peter and the flight of all the disciples (vv. 31-36). But Matthew is more explicit about Jesus' self-gift for fragile disciples. Unlike either Mark or Luke, to the words over the cup, and the passing of the cup as "the blood of the covenant," Matthew adds: "which is poured out for many, *for the forgiveness of sins*" (v. 28). The theme of the forgiveness of sinners, implicit in the Markan account of the Last Supper, has been made explicit in Matthew's account.

(b) The Gospel of Luke

The theme of a "journey" is important across the Gospel of Luke and the Acts of the Apostles.[4] Throughout the Gospel, a journey leads to Jerusalem, where the paschal events take place (see the journey theme across Luke 9:51–19:44). In his account of Jesus' final meal with his disciples (22:14-38), set in Jerusalem, Luke presents this moment as part of a broader missionary setting. The institution narrative does not

---

4   For a more extensive treatment of what follows, see Moloney, *Body Broken*, 144-65.

dominate the passage, devoted mainly to preparing the disciples for the missionary journey that lies ahead of them.

Largely following Mark (see Mark 14:12-16), Luke reports Jesus' preparations for the meal (Luke 22:7-13). He then tells of the shared bread and the shared cup, the body given for the disciples and the blood of a new covenant (vv. 14-20) in an account closer to Paul 11:23-25 than the Markan and the Matthean version. Like Paul, after the gift of the bread, he commands: "Do this in memory of me" (v. 19). Unlike Mark and Matthew, where the meal lies at the center of a carefully structured report of Jesus' final evening with his disciples (Mark 14:22-26; Matt 26:26-29), Luke's account of the meal serves as an introduction to a long "farewell discourse." It is taken for granted as the launching pad for Jesus' preparation of his disciples for their future mission. The rest of Luke's account of this final evening at table prepares his disciples for their future mission, to be pursued in his absence. He predicts the disciples' future challenges. He insists that greatness is found in humble service (vv. 24-30), predicts Simon Peter's denials – and his leadership (vv. 31-34) – and he tells them of their future mission, warning them to be prepared for all that lies ahead (vv. 35-38).[5] As Jesus has foretold, he suffers, dies, rises, and returns to the Father from Jerusalem (see Luke 9:51; 22:47–24:53). His journey has come to an end. An account that began in the Jerusalem Temple with Zechariah (1:5-23), ends in the Jerusalem Temple with the disciples "continually in the temple blessing God" (24:52-53).

At the beginning of the Acts of the Apostles, the first Christian community is still in Jerusalem. There the Spirit is given to the community, and a second journey begins, reaching out to the ends

---

5   For a detailed study upon the missionary nature of Luke's version of Jesus' final meal with his disciples, see Francis J. Moloney, "Luke 22:14-38: Eucharist and Mission," in *Gospel Interpretation and Christian Life*, Scholars Collection 3 (Adelaide: ATF Theology, 2017), 171-89.

of the earth. As we have seen, the city of Jerusalem is the center of God's history.[6] The early Church was founded in that city, the Holy Spirit was given there, and from there a mission began which would reach out to the ends of the earth (see Luke 24:46-49; Acts 1:8). But as the Gospel closes, there is a further journey that is transformed by a Eucharistic encounter.

In the opening remarks of the journey to Emmaus (24:13-35), in the midst of the paschal events, two disciples are going to Emmaus, "about sixty stadia *away from Jerusalem*" (v. 13). They are walking away from Jerusalem, the central point of God's story, away from God's design of the journey of the Son of God from Nazareth to Jerusalem, and of the Christian community from Jerusalem to the ends of the earth. They tell him of their expectations: "We had hoped that he was the one to redeem Israel" (v. 21). Jesus' way of responding to the design of God (see vv. 25-27) has not fulfilled their expectations of the one who would redeem Israel. They know of his life: Jesus of Nazareth, a prophet mighty in word and deed (v. 19). They know of his death: "Our chief priests and rulers delivered him up to be condemned to death, and crucified him" (v. 20). They know of the events at the tomb: "it is now the third day" (v. 21), women have been at the tomb early in the morning, but "they did not find his body" (v. 23). They have even heard the Easter proclamation: there has been a vision of angels who said: "He is alive" (v. 23). The two disciples know everything ... but him they did not see, and thus they have had enough. They continue their walk away from Jerusalem.

Jesus "interpreted to them in all the scriptures the things concerning himself" (v. 27). At the meal they recognized him in the breaking of the bread (vv. 30-31). Jesus followed, joined, and journeyed with these disappointed disciples, as they walked away from God's design. He

---

6   See above, pp. 80-81.

has come to meet them, to make himself known to them and to draw them back to the journey of God through opening the word of God to them, and through the breaking of the bread. Touched in their failure, the immediate reaction of the failed disciples is to turn back on their journey: "And they rose that same hour and returned to Jerusalem" (v. 33). Once they arrive back they are told: "The Lord has risen indeed and has appeared to Simon!" (v. 34).

They have come back home, but only because the Lord has reached out to them and made himself known to them in the breaking of the bread, as they walked away. Now they can be part of the Christian mission, beginning in Jerusalem, and reaching out to the ends of the earth (Acts 1:8). As with Mark, and also with Matthew who has repeated Mark's story (Matt 26:17-35), the Evangelist Luke has no hesitation in setting the Eucharistic presence of the Lord in the midst of the broken disciples. As with Paul, in his rendition of Jesus' final Eucharistic evening with his disciples he instructs them: "Do this in memory of me" (Luke 22:19).

The Gospel of John

In John 13:1-38 Jesus' unconditional self-gift to fragile disciples reaches its most theological expression.[7] The footwashing and its aftermath (vv. 1-17) lead to words from Jesus (vv. 18-20). These words are followed by the gift of the morsel and its aftermath (vv. 21-38). In the footwashing (vv. 1-17) Jesus shows his love for his disciples in his gift of himself for them and in the gift of his example to them (v. 15). The passage highlights his knowledge of the ways of God (v. 3), and his knowledge of all that is about to happen (v. 11). This series of gracious gifts of Jesus to his disciples is contrasted by the themes of the betrayer (vv. 2, 10-11), and the ignorance of the disciples (vv. 6-10).

---

7   See Moloney, *Body Broken*, 175-203.

The gift of the morsel (vv. 21-38) reflects the gifts of the Eucharist and the new commandment (vv. 34-35). There is the repeated reference to the betrayer (vv. 21-26a), the theme of the ignorance of the disciples (vv. 26b-29), the exit of Judas for the betrayal (v. 30) and the prophecy of the denial of Peter (vv. 36-38). Repeating the argument of vv. 1-17 in vv. 21-38, we find Jesus' love for his disciples in the gift of the Eucharistic morsel, and the gift of the new commandment of love, set in the midst of the ignorance of the disciples, the denial of Peter and the betrayal of Judas. To failing disciples Jesus has insisted: "I have given you an example, that you should also do as I have done to you" (v. 15), and "A new commandment I give to you, that you love one another as I have loved you" (v. 34).

At the center of this startling presentation of unconditional love given to failing disciples, in vv. 18-20, we find the key to the passage.

> I am not speaking of you all; I know whom I have chosen: it is that the scripture may be fulfilled, "He who ate my bread has lifted his heel against me."
>
> I tell you this now before it takes place, that when it does take place you may believe that I AM.
>
> Truly, truly, I say to you, he who receives anyone whom I send receives me; and he who receives me receives him who sent me.

The Fourth Evangelist has deliberately set vv. 18-20 between two flanking passages (vv. 1-17 and vv. 21-38). In v. 18 Jesus indicates that he has no illusions about the ones whom he has chosen. One of the them will become the betrayer who has shared in the Eucharistic morsel and another will deny him. Nevertheless, in v. 20 Jesus speaks of his intention to send forth his disciples.

John 13:1-38 is marked by the extraordinary love of God, revealed in Jesus, who gives himself in the footwashing and the Eucharistic morsel. He knows whom he has chosen; he is aware that one who shares his table will betray him, another will deny him and that all the others are unable to understand him, yet he loves them and sends them out to proclaim both himself and his Father. The theological significance of this message is summed up in the central statement of the whole of 13:1-38: "I tell you this now before it takes place, that when it does take place you may believe that I AM" (v. 19). Jesus loves his own so much that he chooses them (v. 18a), and sends them out as his presence (v. 20). Yet, these very loved ones are responsible for his death on a cross (v. 18b). It is precisely in this unconditional gift of himself to people who do not love him that he reveals who he is.

The Fourth Evangelist uses the expression "I am," an expression with a long history in the literature of Israel, to refer to the living presence of a God who is made known among the people, and applies it to the person of Jesus. John informs his readers that only when love reveals itself in such an extraordinary fashion, loving "to the end" (13:1) those who do not love him, can one begin to understand the God whom Jesus has come to make known. When his disciples have betrayed, denied and abandoned him, and he is "lifted up" on the Cross (see 3:13; 8:28; 12:32), then his disciples of all times will know that Jesus is the revelation of God: "I tell you this now, before it takes place, that when it does take place you may believe that I AM" (v. 19).

MISSION

This sketch of some New Testament presentations of the Eucharist does not pretend to exhaust all the possible nuances of the New Testament record. Even less does it pretend to touch upon the rich theological, liturgical, symbolic, cultural and ritual developments of the Church's understanding and celebration of the Eucharist as it has developed and emerged over two thousand years of Christian history. What has been outlined in Paul, the Synoptic Gospels and John, however, speaks clearly to the Eucharistic nature of the Christian mission.

The New Testament's use of the traditions that surrounded the Eucharistic thought and practice of Jesus and the earliest Church reflects *at least* the following convictions:

- The Eucharist is a gift of God, given in and through the death and resurrection of his Son, Jesus Christ (Mark 14:22-24; Matt 26:26-28; Luke 22:19-21; John 6:51c; 1 Cor 11:24-25).

- It is never an end in itself. In all New Testament traditions, the Eucharist is "for" (*hyper*) others. It is never regarded as a purely cultic act, as it is intrinsically associated with the lifestyle of those who participate in the celebration.

- The Eucharist provides access to the saving power of the death and resurrection of Jesus, something that is needed by all who frequent the Lord's table. All the New Testament narratives insist that the Eucharist is for the fragile and the broken, the unique symbol of Jesus' manifestation of God's endless love (John 13:1).

- The celebration of the Eucharist summons participants to break their own bodies and spill their own blood "in memory" of Jesus. "As often as *you* eat this bread and drink the cup, *you* proclaim the Lord's death until he comes" (1 Cor 11:26). Participation in Eucharist demands a Eucharistic and missionary lifestyle, until the end of time.

- It serves as the lived experience of two great gifts: Jesus' example of self-gift that all who claim to be followers of Jesus are to follow (John 13:15) and the gift of the new commandment of mutual love (John 13:34-35).

The Church is God's priestly people (see Rev 1:5-6; 5:10). All the baptized, whatever their sociocultural and political status, have been called to the perfection of love (see *Lumen Gentium* 39-42, especially 40; Pope Francis, *Gaudete et Exsultate* 6-24). Like the Christians at Corinth, and the disciples in the Gospels, we must recognize our brokenness. We are "wounded healers," on a shared Eucharistic journey toward the Parousia. Herein lies the theological and pastoral reason for our mission to others. Eucharist is not primarily a cultic ritual, but a way of life, breaking one's body and spilling one's blood, in memory of Jesus, until he comes again (see 1 Cor 11:26; *Sacrosanctum Concilium* 48).

Our *primary* mission is to those most in need; those reaching out for God's goodness, love and forgiveness. This element of our mission can often be hard to grasp, as just who the most poor and who the "needy" might be cannot always be determined with measurable social and economic criteria. The hunger for the transcendent is a genuine poverty that crosses all ages and all social, ethnic, religious and economic boundaries. There is a sense of "need" in many of these situations. It is such hunger that our Eucharistic ministry must serve, not only in ritual, but above all by the our acceptance that Eucharist is not a prayer wheel that we spin every morning, and more solemnly on Sundays. It is not only cult; but above all a way of life, the grammar of a Christian life.

As that is the case, the traditional *missio ad Gentes* retains its urgency. The baptized are called to give of themselves so that others may have life. The *missio ad Gentes* begins in the Eucharistic nourishment of those sent out on mission. It strives to culminate its activity in the inclusion of others at the Eucharistic table. This aspect of the Christian Eucharist was a further reason for the declaration at the Second Vatican Council that the Eucharist was the "source and summit" of Christian life (*Lumen Gentium* 11. See also *Sacrosanctam Concilium* 2).

No doubt other aspects of the New Testament's presentation of the Eucharist and its central role in "remembering" Jesus, continuing his missionary presence among us that we may have life, could further enrich our reflections upon our mission *ad intra* and *ad Gentes*. Developments in our Eucharistic theology and practice over the ages, in culturally diverse situations where a Spirit-guided Church is present, must play their part for an understanding of the motives and practices of the Christian mission. However, where one starts a journey, and the road one takes, will shape all that follows. The Christian mission had its beginnings in Jesus of Nazareth, whose "remembrance" is celebrated in the Eucharistic life of the Church: "Do this in remembrance of me" (1 Cor 11:24-25; Luke 22:19). It should be at all times nourished and renewed there.

EPILOGUE

Beginning with Jesus of Nazareth, mission has always been central to the religious phenomenon of Christianity. The bulk of the reflections in this study are focused upon the vocations of all who regard themselves as "followers" of Jesus Christ (see Mark 1:16-20) to exercise a missionary activity. For most, this is a vocation to witness to their Christian beliefs and values in their day-to-day lives in their own locality, society, culture and nation. This is often given the Latin description: *missio ad intra*: a mission to ourselves and our own communities, Christian, non-Christian, and increasingly secular. More spectacularly, and often more heroically, from the earliest Christian records (St. Paul is the outstanding example), Christians have journeyed to foreign lands and cultures, bringing the message of the Gospel with them. The technical expression for this activity is *missio ad Gentes*: a mission to non-Christians.

Reflection upon the requirements for mission, especially *ad Gentes*, in these first decades of the third Christian millennium, suggests that more than a biblical study is required. The formation of missionaries must embrace many disciplines: anthropology, comparative religions, understanding cultures, the interface between faith and culture, the acceptance of God's presence in the non-Christian religions, not to speak of the language skills and the psychological balance (and all that entails) required to communicate the Gospel in the missionary's non-native land. The uniformity generated by the Hellenistic Greek world of the earliest Church, gradually expanding to the Latin world of the Roman Empire, no longer exists. Formation for mission *must* recognize the diversity that lies at the center of contemporary society, especially in the post-Christian West. Neglecting the above disciplines, and other critical elements in the human and psychological formation of the prospective missionary, risks the future happiness of the candidate.[1]

The call to be "witnesses to the ends of the earth" (see Luke 24:47-49; Acts 1:8), however, has its roots in Jesus of Nazareth, described by John as the one sent by God that humankind might have life (see John 3:16-17). He was aware in his own time that he was on a mission: "Let us go on to the neighboring towns so that I may proclaim the message there also, for that is what I came out to do" (Mark 1:38). His urgent desire to proclaim the reigning presence of God (see Mark 1:14-15) responded to the design of the God whom he called "Father" (Mark 14:36). This is the bedrock upon which the Christian mission is founded: "'As the Father has sent me, so I send you.' When he had said this, he breathed on them and said to them, 'Receive the Holy Spirit'" (John 20:21-22. See Luke 24:46-49; Acts 1:8).

Our reflections cannot replace the required human formation that a contemporary missionary must receive. However, they provide us with critical reflections on the inspired Word of God, indicating why the Christian mission is so central to Christian existence. We have not exhausted all the New Testament's teachings and allusions to the mission of Jesus and of his disciples. That would require a much larger study, and would not be suitable for the "seminar" situations

---

[1] Sadly, some religious institutions neglect the need for these lengthy and challenging aspects in the formation of *ad Gentes* missionary candidates. It is not enough that the candidate express a desire to be a missionary and be a person of good will. The world receiving contemporary missionaries has changed radically from the world that received them during the "golden years" of European missionaries in the nineteenth and twentieth centuries (not to speak of the first century!). Holiness, hard work, and good will are not enough.

that generated what we have shared.[2] What we have seen, however, provides insights into the theme of the development of a missionary consciousness as an essential element of Christianity, from the time of Jesus to the present.

Paul's insistence that he is driven by a passion that was fired by "the power of the resurrection" (Phil 3:10) is shared by all New Testament witnesses. The association of the disciples with the mission of Jesus in the Gospels (see, for example, Mark 3:13-14; 6:6b-30; Matt 10:1–11:1; Luke 6:14-16; 10:1-12, 17-24; 13:18, 20; 17:9-19) sets a pattern for their post-resurrection continuation, even unto death, of Jesus' preaching the reigning presence of God, and of Jesus as the one sent by God as the bringer of that kingdom (see, for example, Mark 1:14-15; Matt 4:12-17; 9:35; Luke 4:16-20; John 3:16-17). The Christian mission begins with the resurrection commissions, found in all four Gospels. The young man in Mark promises that it will be born when they see the risen Jesus in Galilee (Mark 16:7). For Matthew, the Eleven assemble at the mountain in Galilee, and are sent out to all the nations (Matt 28:16-20). For Luke, Jerusalem is the end point in the life of Jesus, as he returns to the Father. But the risen Jesus promises that a further Spirit-filled and directed missionary journey is about to begin. The gift of the Holy Spirit, the power of the Most High (Luke 24:46-49; Acts 1:6-11) will lead them through failure, rejection, sinfulness, and suffering, to the ends of the earth (Luke 24:47; Acts 1:8). Continuing Jesus' journey, a further missionary journey begins from Jerusalem and will take the disciples to the ends of the earth (Luke 24:47; Acts 1:8). John presents the post-Easter Jesus giving the Holy Spirit to the disciples assembled in the upper room. They are now sent ones of the Father, as Jesus was sent by the Father (John 20:20-21).

---

[2] See the fine volume of Senior and Stuhlmueller, *The Biblical Foundations for Mission*.

Mission only makes sense in the light of the risen Christ. In Luke's Gospel, typical of that author's interest in mission, the two men in dazzling clothes command the women who have come to the tomb on Easter morning to go elsewhere: "Why do you look for the living among the dead? He is not here but has risen" (Luke 24:5). The risen Christ will not be found in graveyards, but in his never-ending presence among those who believe that "he is alive!" (see 24:34).

Perhaps the most significant New Testament scholar of the twentieth century, Rudolf Bultmann, once claimed that Jesus Christ rises in the Church's proclamation. Many have reacted to this point of view angrily, understanding it as a denial of the physical resurrection of Jesus as an explanation of the empty tomb. This is an unjust assessment of Bultmann's position. He claimed (which many would deny) that we simply do not have enough evidence to be *certain* about *what actually happened* on Easter morning. One thing we do know is that from that time on Christians have proclaimed that Jesus is alive, and the experience of the living Jesus among them is confirmation of that truth. This great truth is beautifully caught in the Greek Orthodox traditional Easter greeting: "*Christos anēsti*! – Christ is risen!," to which a fellow-Christian responds "*alēthōs anēsti*! – He is truly risen!

Whatever we make of scholarly discussions of what may or may not have happened to generate an identifiable empty tomb … the faith we proclaim does not depend upon a hole in the ground. Living and proclaiming the lordship of the risen Christ, with the guidance and protection of his Spirit, we set out on mission. However bleak the situation may often appear, nothing can resist the unstoppable energy of the Spirit-driven Christian mission. The risen Jesus will be with us till the end of all the ages (see Matt 28:20). Our mission, proclaiming Jesus Christ as our risen Lord, ensures that Rudolf Bultmann's intuition is correct. We do not believe in Jesus because of an empty tomb; we believe because for two thousand years Jesus has been proclaimed as our risen Christ, and this proclamation rings true. Whatever happened on that first Easter day, Jesus Christ continues to rise in the Church's missionary proclamation.[3]

A significant element in the message of the Gospel of Mark, present to a lesser extent in the other Gospels, is the frailty of the disciples in the period *before* the resurrection of Jesus. Commissioned to do what Jesus has done (Mark 3:13-14), they run the danger that they will forget that a successful mission results from "being with him" (3:14). Once disciples think that their mission is a success because of their own talents and hard work, then they can no longer claim to be missionaries of Jesus Christ (6:30). As the risen Christ commissions his disciples to go to the ends of the earth in the Gospel of Matthew, "some still doubted" (Matt 28:17). Subsequent to the promise of the Spirit and the mission to the ends of the earth in the Gospel and the Acts of the Apostles, at Jesus' ascension to his Father, the disciples stand still, gazing into the sky. They are warned by two men in white: "Men of Galilee, why do you stand looking up toward heaven? This Jesus, who has been taken from you into heaven, will come in the same way as you saw him go into heaven" (Acts 1:11). There is a mission to pursue to the ends of the earth. Gazing into heaven does not advance that mission. The silence of the women, reported in Mark 16:8, makes it clear that a mission that has its beginnings in an encounter with the risen Christ does not depend upon us – he is going before us into Galilee. There we will see him, and with him journey further.

The resurrection account in the Gospel of John also reflects a gradual growth in faith from failure to belief among the founding figures of the earliest Christian community. Mary Magdalene, Peter

---

[3] See Rudolf Bultmann and Five Critics, *Kerygma and Myth*, ed. Hans Werner Bartsch, trans. Reginald Fuller (New York: Harper and Row, 1961), 38-43, especially p. 41. On discussions surrounding the historicity of an empty tomb, see Moloney, *The Resurrection of the Messiah*, 138-48.

and the Beloved Disciple, and Thomas, do not believe (John 20:1-2, 11-15 [Mary]; 20:2 [Peter and the Beloved Disciple]; 20:24-25 [Thomas]). They advance through hope, (20:16-17 [Mary]; 20:3-7 [Peter and the Beloved Disciple]; 20:27 [Thomas]), into unconditional faith (20:18 [Mary]; 20:8 [Beloved Disciple]; 20:28 [Thomas]). John 20 is a powerful reflection upon what the risen Jesus does for his disciples, rather than an account of what happened to Jesus at the resurrection.[4] Encounter with the risen Jesus – in all ages – leads to faith-filled mission.

The consistency of this Gospel message of sinfulness, doubt, and failure in mission also explains Jesus' important instructions to his disciples on the way they should behave as disciples: what they should wear and carry as they pursue their missionary tasks, and the way they should behave once they arrive in their mission. They are to put their lives where their words are. They must practice what they preach (Mark 6:8-13; 10:1-11, 14; Luke 9:1-6). These instructions, shaped by each of the evangelists to speak to their particular situation, indicate that the post-Easter mission was sometimes exercised selfishly or for self-promotion. By telling these stories the Word of God speaks to us in our failures. As those who began their mission in the company of Jesus failed to understand, betrayed and denied him (see John 13:1-38), and held back when they were frightened by the challenge, so do we. Like them, we have been chosen and sent by Jesus. Whoever receives us, receives Jesus, and the one who sent him (see John 13:18-20). The Gospel of John insists that God's love, incarnated in Jesus Christ, has no limits. He loves his own "to the end" (13:1). We have no cause to lose courage and hope, despite our human weaknesses and sinfulness. Jesus goes before us, and will meet us in our mission (see Mark 16:7; Luke 24:13-35); he will be with us always (see Matt

---

4 For a more detailed study of John 20, see Moloney, *The Resurrection of the Messiah*, 106-17.

28:20); he has passed on his Spirit so that our sending matches his (John 20:21), and he will one day come back from heaven, just as he ascended to heaven (Acts 1:11).

The Word of God, proclaimed and heard in the missionary communities of Paul, Mark, Matthew, Luke, and John offered firm indications on the call to preach God's reigning presence, the saving ministry, death and resurrection of Jesus Christ, and a Christian life that imitated the life of Jesus. As Paul would put it: "It is no longer I who live, but it is Christ who lives in me. And the life I now live in the flesh I live by faith in the Son of God who loved me and gave himself for me" (Gal 2:20). The author of the First Letter of John makes the same point, but more directly: "Whoever says 'I abide in him' ought to walk just as he walked" (1 John 2:6).

Jesus' loving self-gift for us (see Gal 2:20; Mark 10:45; John 3:16) is celebrated every time we break bread and share the cup "in memory" of Jesus. The Hebrew and Greek words behind our English word "memory" (Hebrew: *zikkarōn*; Greek: *anamnēsis*) mean more than a misty recollection of an event from the past. In both the Hebrew celebration of the Passover, and the Christian celebration of the Eucharist, which depends for its theology and ritual upon its Hebrew predecessor, those celebrating look back to God's saving actions in the past in a way *that renders them present in the celebration of the Passover and the Eucharist.* For the Hebrew celebration, the events "remembered" are the first "passing over" from the slavery of Egypt to the freedom a new people of God, founded at Sinai. This "Passover" is rendered present at the annual Passover Meal. In the Christian Eucharist, Jesus' death and resurrection are "remembered," rendered present. Jesus addresses all who celebrate: "This is my body, broken for you; this is my blood, shed for you. Will you break your bodies and shed your blood 'in memory of me?'" We respond "Amen" to Jesus' request. In doing so, we commit ourselves to his mission, we proclaim the Lord's death and resurrection until he comes again (paraphrasing 1 Cor 11:23-26). The traditional form of dismissal from the celebration of the Eucharist, retained in our current English translations, sends us on our way: "Go forth, the Mass has ended" (*Ite, missa est!*).[5] Eucharist is not only the central cultic action in the Catholic Tradition; it is the grammar of our lives; it lies at the heart of our missionary vocation.

---

5   The same intention is found in other words of dismissal found in the current *Roman Missal*: "Go and announce the Gospel of the Lord," and "Go in peace, glorifying the Lord by your life."

BIBLIOGRAPHY

Commentaries

Beasley-Murray, George R. *John*. Word Biblical Commentary 36. Waco, TX: Word Books, 1987.

Brown, Raymond E. *The Death of the Messiah: From Gethsemane to the Grave: A Commentary on the Passion Narrative of the Four Gospels*. 2 vols. Anchor Bible Reference Library. New York: Doubleday, 1994.

――――――. *The Gospel According to John*. Anchor Bible 29-29A. 2 vols. Garden City: Doubleday, 1966-1970.

Byrne, Brendan. *Romans*. Sacra Pagina 6. Collegeville: Liturgical Press, 1996.

Carroll, John T. *Luke. A Commentary*. The New Testament Library. Louisville: Westminster John Knox, 2012.

Collange, Jean-François. *The Epistle of Saint Paul to the Philippians*. Translated by A. W. Heathcote. London: Epworth Press, 1979.

Davies, William D., and Dale C. Allison. *The Gospel According to Saint Matthew*. 3 vols. International Critical Commentary. Edinburgh: T. & T. Clark, 1988-1997.

Dunn, James D. G. *Romans*. 2 vols. Word Biblical Commentary 38a-b. Dallas, TX: Word Books, 1988.

Fitzmyer, Joseph A. *The Acts of the Apostles*. Anchor Bible 31. New York: Doubleday, 1998.

Hooker, Morna D. *The Gospel According to Saint Mark*. Black's New Testament Commentaries. London: A. & C. Black, 1991.

Hoskyns, Edwyn C. *The Fourth Gospel*. Edited by Francis N. Davey. London: Faber & Faber, 1947.

Johnson, Luke T. *The Acts of the Apostles*. Sacra Pagina 5. Collegeville: Liturgical Press, 1992.

_____. *The Gospel of Luke*. Sacra Pagina 3. Collegeville: Liturgical Press, 1991.

_____. *The Letter of James*. Anchor Bible 37a. New York: Doubleday, 1995.

Luz, Ulrich. *Matthew*. Translated by James E. Crouch. 3 vols. Hermeneia. Minneapolis: Fortress, 2001-2007.

Meier, John P. *Matthew*. New Testament Message 3. Wilmington, DE: Michael Glazier, 1980.

Moloney, Francis J. *Glory not Dishonor. Reading John 13-21*. Minneapolis: Fortress, 1998.

_____. *The Gospel of John*. Sacra Pagina 4. Collegeville: Liturgical Press, 1998.

_____. *The Gospel of Mark. A Commentary*. Grand Rapids: Baker Academic, 2012.

Parsons, Mikeal C. *Acts*. Paideia Commentaries on the New Testament. Grand Rapids: Baker Academic, 2008.

Schweizer, Eduard. *The Good News According to Mark*. Translated by Donald H. Madvig. London: SPCK, 1971.

———. *The Good News According to Matthew*. Translated by David E. Green. London: SPCK, 1976.

Senior, Donald. *Matthew*. Abingdon New Testament Commentaries. Nashville, TN: Abingdon, 1998.

Other Works

Babylonian Talmud. Translated and edited by Isidore Epstein. 35 vols. London: Soncino, 1948-1952.

Blass, Friedrich A., Albert Debrunner, and Robert W. Funk. *A Greek Grammar of the New Testament and Other Early Christian Literature*. Chicago: Chicago University Press, 1961.

Brown, Raymond E. *An Introduction to the New Testament*. Anchor Bible Reference Library. New York: Doubleday, 1997.

Brown, Sherri, and Francis J. Moloney. *Interpreting the New Testament. An Introduction*. Grand Rapids: Eerdmans, 2019.

Bultmann, Rudolf, and Five Critics. *Kerygma and Myth*. Edited by Hans Werner Bartsch. Translated by Reginald H. Fuller. New York: Harper and Row, 1961.

Byrne, Brendan. "A Pauline Complement to *Laudato Sì*." *Theological Studies* 77 (2016): 308-27.

———. "Christ's Pre-Existence in Pauline Soteriology." *Theological Studies* 58 (1997): 308-30.

———. "Interpreting Romans Theologically in a Post – 'New Perspective' Perspective." *Harvard Theological Review* 94 (2001): 227-41.

---------. *Reckoning with Romans. A Contemporary Reading of Paul's Gospel.* Good News Studies 18. Wilmington, DE: Michael Glazier, 1986.

---------. "The Problem of *Nomos* and the Relationship with Judaism in Romans." *The Catholic Biblical Quarterly* 62 (2000): 294-309.

Charlesworth, James H. *The Old Testament Pseudepigrapha.* 2 vols. New York: Doubleday, 1985.

Chatman, Seymour. *Story and Discourse. Narrative Structure in Fiction and Film.* Ithaca, NY: Cornell University Press, 1978.

Chennattu, Rekha M. *Johannine Discipleship as a Covenant Relationship.* Peabody, MA: Hendrickson, 2006.

Chryssavgis, John. *Repentance and Confession in the Orthodox Church.* Brookline, MA: The Holy Cross Orthodox Press, 2004.

Conzelmann, Hans. *The Theology of St. Luke.* Translated by Geoffrey Buswell. London: Faber & Faber, 1960.

Culpepper, R. Alan. *John, the Son of Zebedee. The Life of a Legend.* Studies on Personalities of the New Testament. Columbia, SC: University of South Carolina Press, 1994.

Danby, Herbert. *The Mishnah. Translated from the Hebrew with Brief Expanatory Notes.* Oxford: Oxford University Press, 1938.

Danker, Frederick W. *A Greek-English Lexicon of the New Testament and Other Early Christian Literature.* Chicago: Chicago University Press, 2000.

Dix, Gregory. *The Apostolic Tradition of Hippolytus of Rome*. London: SPCK, 1937.

Dunne, James D. G. *The New Perspective on Paul*. Revised edition. Grand Rapids: Eerdmans, 2008.

Edwards, James R. "Marcan Sandwiches: The Significance of Interpolations in Marcan Narratives." *Novum Testamentum* 31 (1989): 193-216.

Eire, Carlos M. N. *Reformations. The Early Modern World 1450–1650*. New Haven: Yale University Press, 2016.

Falls, Thomas B. *Saint Justin Martyr. The First Apology, The Second Apology, Dialogue with Trypho, Exhortation to the Greeks, Discourse to the Greeks, The Monarchy or the Rule of God*. The Fathers of the Church. Washington, DC: The Catholic University of America Press, 1948.

Flannery, Austin. *Vatican Council II. The Conciliar and Postconciliar Documents*. New Revised Edition. Collegeville: Liturgical Press, 1996.

Fitzmyer, Joseph A. "*Kyrios*." Volume 2, pages 328-31 in *Exegetical Dictionary of the New Testament*. Edited by Horst Balz and Gerhard Schneider. Grand Rapids: Eerdmans, 1991.

_____. "The Ascension of Christ and Pentecost." *Theological Studies* 45 (1984): 409-40.

Francis, Pope. *Evangelii Gaudium. Apostolic Exhortation on the Proclamation of the Gospel in Today's World*. Vatican City: Libreria Editrice Vaticana, 2013.

_____. *Gaudete et Exsultate. Apostolic Exhortation on the Call to Holiness in Today's World*. Vatican City: Libreria Editrice Vaticana, 2018.

———. *Laudato Sì. An Encyclical Letter on Ecology and Climate.* Vatican City: Libreria Editrice Vaticana, 2015.

Furnish, Victor P. *The Love Command in the New Testament.* London: SCM Press, 1973.

Goodman, Martin. *A History of Judaism.* London: Allen Lane, 2017.

Hare, Douglas, and Daniel Harrington. "'Make Disciples of all the Gentiles' (Matt 28:19)." Pages 110-23 in *Light of all Nations. Essays in the Church in New Testament Research.* Good News Studies 3. Wilmington, DE: Michael Glazier, 1982.

Harris, Horton. *The Tübingen School.* Oxford: Clarendon Press, 1975.

Hengel, Martin. *Crucifixion.* London: SCM Press, 1977.

Holmes, Michael W. *The Apostolic Fathers. Greek Texts and English Translations.* 3rd ed. Grand Rapids: Baker Academic, 2007.

Horrell, David G. *An Introduction to the Study of Paul.* 2nd ed. London: T. & T. Clark, 2006.

Iverson, Kelly R., and Christopher W. Skinner, eds. *Mark as Story. Retrospect and Prospect.* Society of Biblical Literature Resources for Biblical Study 65. Atlanta: Society for Biblical Study, 2011.

Kelly, J. N. D. *Jerome. His Life, Writings, and Controversies.* Peabody, MA: Hendrickson, 2000.

Kurz, William. *Farewell Addresses in the New Testament.* Zacchaeus Studies: New Testament. Wilmington, DE: Michael Glazier, 1990.

Marcus, Joel. "Mark – Interpreter of Paul." *New Testament Studies* 46 (2000): 473-87.

Martin, Ralph P. *Carmen Christi. Philippians ii. 5-11 in Recent Interpretation and in the Setting of Early Christian Worship.* Society for New Testament Studies Monograph Series 4. Cambridge: Cambridge University Press, 1967.

Meier, John P. *A Marginal Jew. Rethinking the Historical Jesus.* 5 vols. The Anchor Yale Bible Reference Library. New York/New Haven: Doubleday/Yale University Press, 1991-2016.

_____. *Law and History in Matthew's Gospel.* Analecta Biblica 71. Rome: Biblical Institute Press, 1976.

_____. "Nations or Gentiles in Mt 28:19." *Catholic Biblical Quarterly* 39 (1997): 94-102.

_____. *The Vision of Matthew: Christ, Church and Morality in the First Gospel.* Theological Inquiries. New York: Paulist, 1978.

Moloney, Francis J. *A Body Broken for a Broken People. Divorce, Remarriage, and the Eucharist.* 3rd ed. Mulgrave, VIC: John Garratt, 2015.

_____. "A New Testament Hermeneutic for Divorce and Remarriage in the Catholic Tradition." *The Australasian Catholic Record* 93 (2016): 269-88.

_____. *Broken for You. Jesus Christ, the Catholic Priesthood & the Word of God.* Bayswater, VIC: Coventry Press, 2018.

_____. *Eucharist as a Celebration of Forgiveness.* New York: Paulist, 2017.

_____. "'For as yet they did not know the Scripture' (John 20:9): A Study in Narrative Time." *The Irish Theological Quarterly* 79 (2014): 97-111.

_____. *Gospel Interpretation and Christian Life.* Scholars Collection 3. Adelaide: ATF Theology, 2017.

_____. "'He is going before you into Galilee.' Mark 16:6-8 and the Christian Community." Pages 117-30 in *Gospel Interpretation and Christian Life*. Scholars Collection 3. Adelaide: ATF Theology, 2017.

_____. *Love in the Gospel of John. An Exegetical, Theological, and Literary Study*. Grand Rapids: Baker Academic, 2015.

_____. "Luke 22:14-38: Eucharist and Mission." Pages 171-89 in *Gospel Interpretation and Christian Life*. Scholars Collection 3. Adelaide: ATF Theology, 2017.

_____. "Mark 6:6b-30: The Twelve, Mission, and Failure." Pages 15-45 in *Gospel Interpretation and Christian Life*. Scholars Collection 3. Adelaide: ATF Theology, 2017.

_____. *Mark: Storyteller, Interpreter, Evangelist*. Peabody, MA: Hendrickson, 2004.

_____. *Reading the New Testament in the Church. A Primer for Pastors, Religious Educators, and Believers*. Grand Rapids: Baker Academic, 2015.

_____. "Sacred Scripture at Vatican II." *Toronto Journal of Theology* 23, no. 2 (2016): 237-48.

_____. "The Fourth Gospel and the Jesus of History." *New Testament Studies* 45 (1999): 42-58.

_____. "The Gospel of Creation. A Biblical Response to Laudato Sì." Pages 259-82 in *Gospel Interpretation and Christian Life*. Scholars Collection 3. Adelaide: ATF Theology, 2017.

_____. *The Living Voice of the Gospel. The Gospels Today*. 2nd ed. Mulgrave, VIC: John Garratt, 2006.

_____. *The Resurrection of the Messiah. A Narrative Commentary on the Resurrection Narratives in the Four Gospels.* New York: Paulist, 2015.

Murphy-O'Connor, Jerome. *St. Paul's Corinth. Texts and Archeology.* Good News Studies 6. Wilmington, DE: Michael Glazier, 1983.

Nouwen, Henri. *The Wounded Healer. Ministry in Contemporary Society.* New York: Doubleday Image Books, 1979.

O'Malley, John W. *Trent. What Happened at the Council.* Cambridge, MA: Harvard University Press, 2013.

_____. *Vatican I. The Council and the Making of the Ultramontane Church.* Cambridge, MA: Harvard University Press, 2018.

Parsons, Mikeal C., and Richard I. Pervo. *Rethinking the Unity of Luke and Acts.* Minneapolis: Fortress, 1993.

Parsons, Mikeal C. *Luke: Storyteller, Interpreter, Evangelist.* Peabody, MA: Hendrickson, 2007.

Powell, Mark A. *Introducing the New Testament: A Historical, Theological, and Literary Survey.* Grand Rapids: Baker Academic, 2009.

Ratzinger, Joseph. *Jesus of Nazareth.* 3 vols. New York/San Francisco: Doubleday/Image/Ignatius Press, 2007-2012.

Rimmon-Kenan, Shlomith. *Narrative Fiction. Contemporary Poetics.* New Accents. London: Methuen, 1983.

Sanders, Ed Parish. *Paul and Palestinian Judaism. A Comparison of Patterns of Religion.* Philadelphia: Fortress, 1977.

Schaberg, Jane. *The Father, the Son and the Holy Spirit. The Triadic Phrase in Matthew 28:19b.* Society of Biblical Literature

Dissertation Series 61. Chico, CA: Scholars Press, 1982.

Schneiders, Sandra M. *Jesus Risen in Our Midst. Essays on the Resurrection in the Fourth Gospel.* Collegeville: Liturgical Press, 2013.

_____. "The Resurrection (of the Body) in the Fourth Gospel: A Key to Johannine Spirituality." Pages 168-98 in *Life in Abundance: Studies in John's Gospel in Tribute to Raymond E. Brown.* Edited by John R. Donahue. Collegeville: Liturgical Press, 2005.

Schweizer, Eduard. "Mark's Theological Achievement." Pages 42-63 in *The Interpretation of Mark.* Edited by William Telford. Issues in Religion and Theology 7. Philadelphia: Fortress, 1985.

Scroggs, Robin. *The Last Adam. A Study in Pauline Anthropology.* Oxford: Basil Blackwell, 1966.

Senior, Donald. *The Passion of Jesus in the Gospel of Matthew.* The Passion Series 1. Wilmington, DE: Michael Glazier, 1985.

Senior, Donald, and Carroll Stuhlmueller. *The Biblical Foundations for Mission.* Maryknoll, NY: Orbis Books, 1983.

Sim, David. *The Gospel of Matthew and Christian Judaism. The History and Social Setting of the Matthean Community.* Studies in the New Testament and Its World. Edinburgh: T. & T. Clark, 1998.

Smith, D. Moody. "When Did the Gospels Become Scripture?" *Journal of Biblical Literature* 119 (2000): 3-20.

Spivey, Robert A., D. Moody Smith, and C. Clifton Black. *Anatomy of the New Testament. A Guide to Its Structure and Meaning.* 7th ed. Minneapolis: Fortress, 2013.

Thackeray, H. St. J., Ralph Marcus, and Louis Feldman. *Josephus.* 9 vols. Loeb Classical Library. London/Cambridge, MA: William Heinemann/Harvard University Press, 1926-1965.

von Campenhausen, Hans. *The Fathers of the Church.* Peabody, MA: Hendrickson, 2000.

Wilkinson, John. "The Incident of the Blood and Water in John 19:34." *Scottish Journal of Theology* 28 (1975): 149-72.

www.ingramcontent.com/pod-product-compliance
Lightning Source LLC
Chambersburg PA
CBHW032258150426
43195CB00008BA/498